Instant Pot Cookbook For Beginners

150 Easy, Delicious, and Healthy Recipes for Your Electric Pressure Cooker

Angela Hopkins

© **Text Copyright 2023 by Angela Hopkins - All rights reserved.**

This document is geared towards providing exact and reliable information in regards to the topic and issue covered. The publication is sold with the idea that the publisher is not required to render accounting, officially permitted, or otherwise, qualified services. If advice is necessary, legal or professional, a practiced individual in the profession should be ordered.

From a Declaration of Principles which was accepted and approved equally by a Committee of the American Bar Association and a Committee of Publishers and Associations.

In no way is it legal to reproduce, duplicate, or transmit any part of this document in either electronic means or in printed format. Recording of this publication is strictly prohibited and any storage of this document is not allowed unless with written permission from the publisher. All rights reserved.

The information provided herein is stated to be truthful and consistent, in that any liability, in terms of inattention or otherwise, by any usage or abuse of any policies, processes, or directions contained within is the solitary and utter responsibility of the recipient reader. Under no circumstances will any legal responsibility or blame be held against the publisher for any reparation, damages, or monetary loss due to the information herein, either directly or indirectly.

Respective authors own all copyrights not held by the publisher.

The information herein is offered for informational purposes solely, and is universal as so. The presentation of the information is without contract or any type of guarantee assurance.

The trademarks that are used are without any consent, and the publication of the trademark is without permission or backing by the trademark owner. All trademarks and brands within this book are for clarifying purposes only and are owned by the owners themselves, not affiliated with this document.

Paperback ISBN: 978-1-64842-552-3

Table of Contents

Introduction 1

CHAPTER ONE

Know Your Instant Pot 3

    What is the Instant Pot? 3
    Benefits of Using the Instant Pot 3
    How to Use an Instant Pot 5
    Tips for Cooking in the Instant Pot 7

CHAPTER TWO

Breakfast 9

    Easy Egg Cups 9
    Cranberry Almond Grits 10
    Eggs and Cheese Casserole 11
    Breakfast Pie 12
    Almonds and Oats 13
    Instant Pot Apple Cranberry Oats 14
    Pumpkin Porridge 15
    Gluten-Free and Vegan Buckwheat Porridge 17
    Blueberry Bowl 18
    Rice Pudding Parfait 19
    Potato Bacon Gratin 20
    Egg Croissants 21
    Sausage and Bacon Frittata 22
    French Toast 23
    No-Crust Quiche 25
    Instant Quinoa 26
    Scrambled Eggs 27
    Eggs in Bell Pepper Cups 28
    Veggie Hash 29

CHAPTER THREE

Poultry 30

    Chicken Teriyaki 30
    Pesto Chicken... 31
    Lemon Coconut Chicken 32
    Duck in Lemon Sauce 33
    Pina Colada Chicken 34
    Chili Chicken...35
    Barbecue Chicken 36
    Cacciatore Chicken 37
    Sweet Garlic Chicken 38
    Cajun Chicken with Rice 39
    Chicken Thighs with Feta Cheese 40
    Chicken Salad.. 41
    Turkey Meatballs 43
    Simple Herb Turkey Breast 44
    Turkey Goulash 45
    Turkey in Orange-Ginger Sauce 46
    Roasted Cornish Hen 47
    Buffalo Chicken..48
    BBQ Chicken Thighs 49
    Chicken and Broccoli 50

CHAPTER FOUR

Meats **52**

    Beef and Beans..52
    Beef Chili with Kale..53
    Beef Bourguignon 54
    Paleo Meatloaf 56
    Pork Chops with Tomatoes 57
    Sesame Beef & Broccoli 58
    Swedish Meatballs 59
    Maple Smoked Brisket 60
    Knorr Demi-Glace Brisket 61
    Mongolian Beef...62
    Ground Beef Tacos..63
    Balsamic Pot Roast 65
    Sweet and Sticky Short Ribs 66
    Instant Pot Pork Vindaloo 67

Pulled Pork Salad 69
Pork Wraps 70
Barbecue Pork Ribs 71
Super Sausage and Peppers 73
Braised Lamb Shanks 74
Garlicky Lamb 75
Rosemary Lamb Chops 76
Flank Steak 77
Feta Meatloaf 78

CHAPTER FIVE

Fish and Seafood 80

Cod with Parsley and Peas 80
Vietnamese Salmon 81
Seafood Gumbo 82
Coconut Fish Curry 83
Tuna Steaks with Capers 85
Shrimp Fried Rice 86
Spicy Shrimp 87
Paprika Shrimp Stew 88
Mediterranean Calamari 89
Orange Salmon 90
Steamed Salmon 91
Fish Chowder 92
Fish Curry 93
Ginger-Lemon Haddock 94
Steamed Mussels 95
Flounder Piccata 96
Fish and Tomatoes 97
Mahi-Mahi in Tomato Sauce 98

CHAPTER SIX

Vegetables and Beans 99

Spiced Okra 99
Vegetable Medley 100
Corn Chowder 101
Creamed Kale 102

Beet Salad 103
  Zucchini with Tomatoes 104
  Brussels Sprout Salad 105
  Lentil Tacos... 106
  Garlicky Bell Peppers 107
  Butternut Squash Risotto 108
  Spinach with Tomatoes.. 109
  Cherry Tomato Cacciatore 110
  Black Beans and Burrito Bowl 111
  Cabbage with Carrot 112
  Garlic Mashed Potatoes 113
  Vegetable Curry 114
  Pumpkin Curry 115
  Spinach with Cheese 116
  Tomato with Tofu 117

CHAPTER SEVEN

Soups, Stews, and Chilis 118

  Beef Stew.. 118
  Chicken Noodle Soup..119
  Broccoli Bacon Soup 120
  Coconut Chicken Soup..121
  Split Pea Soup 122
  High Fiber Vegetable Soup 124
  Cauliflower Potato Soup 125
  Butternut Squash Soup 126
  Lentil Soup.. 127
  Creamy Tomato Soup 128
  Hot and Sour Soup... 129
  Ham and Bean Soup 130
  Minestrone Soup...131
  Beef Barley Soup 132
  Oxtail Soup.. 133
  Chicken and Salsa Soup 134
  Lamb Stew 135
  Mushroom Stew... 136
  Beef & Pork Chili.. 137

Turkey Chili 138

CHAPTER EIGHT

Snacks and Appetizers 139

    Cheesy Spinach Dip 139
    Jalapeño Poppers 140
    Carrot Sticks 141
    Hot Chicken Wings 142
    Creamy Artichoke Dip 143
    Cheese Broccoli Dip 144
    Candied Lemon Peels 145
    Tangy Sweet Potato Wedges 146
    Prosciutto Wrapped Asparagus 147
    Scotch Eggs 148
    Chunky Applesauce 149
    Glazed Pears 150
    Spicy Mushrooms 151

CHAPTER NINE

Dessert 153

    Coconut Rice Pudding 153
    Lemon Coconut Squares 154
    Chocolate Mousse with Raspberries 156
    Green Tea Coconut Crème Brûlée 157
    Pear Applesauce 158
    Cranberry Bread Pudding 159
    Chocolate Pudding 161
    Tapioca Pudding 162
    Molten Chocolate Mini Lava Cakes 163
    Chocolate Cake with Jam 164
    Oreo Cheesecake 165
    Caramel Flan 166
    Apples A La Mode 168
    Chocolate Brownies 169
    Wine Poached Figs on Yogurt Crème 170
    Nutty Fudge Pieces 171
    Homemade Yogurt 172

Blueberry Walnut Porridge.. 173
Conclusion 174

Introduction

Welcome to the "Instant Pot Cookbook for Beginners." Whether you've just brought home your very first Instant Pot or you're simply looking to expand your culinary repertoire, this book will be the perfect companion on your journey.

With the Instant Pot's revolutionary cooking technology, you can say goodbye to long cooking hours and say hello to delicious dishes that won't have you hovering around the kitchen. The 150 recipes in this book will ensure that every meal is a celebration. Each recipe is not just palatable but also brimming with nutrition.

Here's a glimpse of what awaits you:

    Chapter 1: Know Your Instant Pot – Begin your journey with a comprehensive guide to understanding and mastering your Instant Pot.

    Chapter 2: Breakfast Recipes – Start your day right with hearty and energizing morning meals.

    Chapter 3: Poultry Recipes – From juicy chicken to tender turkey, discover a world of poultry delights.

    Chapter 4: Meat Recipes – Enjoy the rich flavors of beef, lamb, pork, and more.

    Chapter 5: Fish and Seafood Recipes – Dive into seafood dishes, from silky salmon to delectable shrimp.

    Chapter 6: Vegetable Recipes – Celebrate the best of plant-based meals, each bursting with vitamins and minerals.

    Chapter 7: Soup Recipes – Find comfort in a bowl with an array of warming concoctions.

    Chapter 8: Snack Recipes – Perfect for those midday munchies or evening get-togethers.

    Chapter 9: Dessert Recipes – Complete your meals on a sweet note with indulgent treats that will leave you craving more.

So, roll up your sleeves, switch on your Instant Pot, and let's embark on this exciting culinary adventure together!

Happy Cooking!

CHAPTER ONE

Know Your Instant Pot

The Instant Pot is not just another kitchen appliance; for many, it's revolutionized the way they approach home-cooking.

What is the Instant Pot?

The Instant Pot is a multifunctional electric pressure cooker that can perform the tasks of several kitchen appliances all in one. At its core, the Instant Pot is a pressure cooker, but with its multiple settings and functionalities, it can also serve as a slow cooker, rice cooker, steamer, yogurt maker, sauté pan, and warmer.

Designed with an inner stainless-steel pot, it uses a combination of heat and pressure to cook food rapidly. The device has a sealed environment, so the heat and pressure are trapped inside, allowing for faster cooking times and more intense flavor absorption.

Benefits of Using the Instant Pot

Cook Faster
Perhaps the most celebrated benefit of the Instant Pot is its ability to significantly reduce cooking time. Foods that typically take hours to cook, like beef stews or beans, can be done in a fraction of the time.

Easy to Use
The menu interface on the front of the Instant Pot has settings that are similar to a microwave oven and are very easy to use. If a recipe calls for searing meat first and then slow cooking it afterward, you can do this easily with the pot. Instant Pot makes it possible for

home cooks to create complex meals in just one pot. For many of us, this also means not having to wash too many pots after dinner. In addition, cleaning the pot is a breeze and you won't need to exert too much effort when scrubbing it down.

An Instant Pot can save kitchen space as you no longer need to have multiple appliances. This means you don't need to have a separate rice cooker, slow cooker, or yogurt maker. The pot does all these things for you. If you're single and you don't do a lot of cooking, this is also a great way to avoid spending lots of money on appliances that you seldom use.

Preservation of the Nutritional Value of Food
The longer you cook food, the more you're cooking off valuable ingredients such as vitamins, minerals, and proteins. Instant Pot cooking will not do that to your food. Since the pot is designed to evenly distribute steam, there is no need to immerse food in water. All you have to do is fill the bottom of the pot with enough water to create steam. This helps tremendously when it comes to preserving nutrients in the food, which water otherwise washes away.

Energy Efficient
Due to its sealed environment and shorter cooking times, the Instant Pot uses up to 70% less energy compared to traditional cooking methods.

How to Use an Instant Pot

Instant Pot Buttons

There are manual settings, as well as a full range of pre-selected cooking routines that you can program with the push of a single button. A timer can even delay the start time for up to 24 hours. Below are the standard buttons that make using the Instant Pot such a pleasure:

MANUAL/PRESSURE COOK: this button is used when you want to adjust the pressure and cooking time. The majority of recipes in this book use the MANUAL or PRESSURE COOK setting.

SAUTÉ: this function sautés and can be adjusted up to **browning** or down to **simmer.** The button is also used to reheat food and to thicken sauces.

SLOW COOK: this button turns the Instant Pot into a slow cooker. When using this setting, you must turn the pressure release handle to the Venting position.

KEEP WARM: this button keeps the food warm.

CANCEL: this button cancels a prior function.

SOUP: this function prepares soups at high pressure for 30 minutes. The time can be manually adjusted by using the "-" or "+" buttons.

MEAT/STEW: this button cooks meats at high pressure for 35 minutes. Cooking time can be adjusted manually.

BEAN/CHILI: this button prepares beans at high pressure for 30 minutes. Cooking time can be adjusted manually.

POULTRY: this button cooks chicken at high pressure for 15 minutes. Cooking time can be adjusted manually.

RICE: this function prepares white rice; the cooking time cannot be adjusted manually.

MULTIGRAIN: this function cooks at high pressure for 40 minutes. Cooking time can be adjusted manually.

PORRIDGE: this function cooks porridge at high pressure for 20 minutes. Cooking time can be adjusted manually.

STEAM: this button is used to steam foods such as vegetables in a steamer basket. It cooks at high pressure for 10 minutes.

Pressure Release Methods

There are two ways to release pressure in an Instant Pot: the "quick pressure release" or the "natural pressure release." The "quick pressure release" happens when the pressure valve is opened manually, and the steam is released quickly. As the steam is released, so is the pressure. When all of the pressure is released, the float valve sinks and the lid is unlocked. For safety's sake, there is no way for the lid to open until the float valve drops. Some steam will be given off, so don't stick your face too close just yet.

The "natural pressure release" happens when you let the pressure decrease without opening the pressure valve. After the allotted cooking time, the Instant Pot automatically switches from cooking mode to the "Keep Warm" mode. During this time, the pressure naturally drops. How long this takes depends on how much liquid is in the pot. It can take anywhere from ten minutes to half an hour. The float valve will drop when it is time.

What specific release method should you use? For vegetables, it is best to use the "quick pressure release," since vegetables will get soggy if overcooked. The "natural pressure release" method is a great way to let meats, soups, and stews simmer.

Tips for Cooking in the Instant Pot

While it does many things with ease, the Instant Pot is especially well-suited for the creation of soups, chilis, and stews made from scratch. Its ability to soften up unsoaked beans, while all the other ingredients cook, is a real bonus for busy people. It can also turn even the toughest cut of meat into fall-off-the-bone perfection in very short order, which makes it ideal for things such as spare ribs. However, certain cuts of meat such as tender steaks are better cooked on a grill. Pasta is also easier to cook using the standard boiling method.

To get the most effective use from your Instant Pot, make sure you use recipes that are specifically designed for this type of cooking tool. Make sure you use enough liquid when you're cooking, and don't try to fry anything in it because oil can damage the system.

Keep it Simple at the Start

It's going to take you a while to familiarize yourself with the variety of functions with which an Instant Pot is equipped. If you are just getting started with your new pot, you need to keep things simple. Rather than trying your hand at a complex recipe, try something easy first, such as boiling eggs, warming up a dish, or your favorite chicken noodle recipe.

Add Extra Time

When referring to an Instant Pot recipe, you may need to add an extra 10 minutes to the cooking time since the pressure cooker needs time to build up heat and pressure. However, you don't need to add cook time if you're using the slow cooker or sauté options. Because of the time lag involved in both starting and stopping the pressure cooking process, fish and seafood have to be treated with particular care since many of these ingredients can turn either mushy or rubbery if overcooked.

Don't Overfill the Instant Pot

A good rule of thumb is to fill your pot only two-thirds of the way, and if making something that is supposed to rise during cooking, fill it only halfway through. Overfilling the pot may contribute to clogging the valve and will increase the pressure significantly.

Don't Use Too Much Liquid

Yes, the Instant Pot needs liquid to build up the pressure. However, keep in mind that too much liquid can dilute the flavor and make your meals bland. Unless the recipe calls otherwise, do not use more than 1½ cups of liquid.

Get Extra Parts

The Instant Pot comes with a stainless steel inner pot. Getting an extra inner pot could help you to prepare two different dishes. Also, if you use the Instant Pot quite often, then you will always have one inner pot available for use while the other is being cleaned in the dishwasher.

You can also cook with different lids. You can get a glass lid, which is similar to a slow cooker lid, and use this lid when you're using the sauté or slow cooker functions. The glass lid cannot be used for the pressure cooking function.

Clean it Regularly

Just because it takes less time to cook, does not mean that an Instant Pot doesn't require frequent cleaning. Fortunately, this appliance is very easy to clean, as the inner pot is easily detachable. Make it a habit to clean your Instant Pot after each use.

Knowing how to use the Instant pot will give you fantastic meals all year long. In the following chapters, you will find 150 easy and healthy Instant Pot recipes for breakfast, poultry, meats, seafood, vegetables, soups, snacks, and dessert.

CHAPTER TWO

Breakfast

Easy Egg Cups

Serves: 4
Preparation Time: 10 minutes
Cooking Time: 13 minutes
Ingredients:
4 ramekins
4 eggs
4 slices ham
4 slices cheese
4 sprigs fresh rosemary
2 teaspoons olive oil
1 cup water

Directions:
1. Pour the water into the Instant Pot. Lightly rub the inside of each ramekin with olive oil.
2. Crack open an egg and add it to a ramekin. Add the ham and then the cheese to the same ramekin. Repeat for each egg.
3. Place the ramekins into a steamer basket and lower into the Instant Pot. Close the lid, choose the MANUAL or PRESSURE COOK setting, and cook at high pressure for 5 minutes.
4. When the cooking is complete, do a natural pressure release for 10 minutes. Quick release the remaining pressure.
5. Remove the ramekins and sprinkle with fresh rosemary.

Nutritional Information (Per Serving)
Calories: 242; Fat: 18.4g; Net Carbohydrates: 1.4g; Protein: 17.2g

Cranberry Almond Grits

Serves: 6
Preparation Time: 10 minutes
Cooking Time: 15 minutes
Ingredients:
1 cup grits
4 cups water
½ teaspoon salt
1 cup dried cranberries
½ cup sliced almonds, toasted
¼ cup milk
1 tablespoon unsalted butter

Directions:

1. Rinse the grits with water and drain. Add the grits, salt, cranberries, and water to the Instant Pot. Mix well.

2. Close the lid, choose the MANUAL or PRESSURE COOK setting, and cook at high pressure for 10 minutes.

3. When the cooking is complete, do a natural pressure release for 10 minutes. Quick release the remaining pressure.

4. Open the lid and stir in the butter and milk. Mix well.

5. Spoon into bowls and sprinkle with the almond slices.

Nutritional Information (Per Serving)
Calories: 165; Fat: 6g; Net Carbohydrates: 27g; Protein: 2g

Eggs and Cheese Casserole

Serves: 6
Preparation Time: 10 minutes
Cooking Time: 20 minutes
Ingredients:
6 large eggs
1 chopped small onion
1 cup diced ham
¼ cup heavy cream
1 cup diced cheddar cheese
1 teaspoon Herbs de Provence
Salt and pepper to taste

Directions:

1. In a bowl, beat the eggs and heavy cream until fluffy. Add the remaining ingredients to the bowl and stir.

2. Place the egg mixture in a heatproof dish; cover the dish with foil.

3. Pour 1 cup of water into the bottom of the Instant pot. Add a steamer rack and place the dish on the rack.

4. Close the lid, press the MANUAL or PRESSURE COOK setting, and cook at high pressure for 20 minutes.

5. When the cooking is complete, do a natural pressure release.

Nutritional Information (Per Serving)
Calories: 206; Fat: 15.0g; Net Carbohydrates: 2.2g; Protein: 15.0g

Breakfast Pie

Serves: 8
Preparation Time: 15 minutes
Cooking Time: 20 minutes
Ingredients:
12 eggs, whisked
1½ pounds breakfast pork sausages, broken
2 sweet potatoes, shredded
1½ tablespoons garlic powder
1 large green bell pepper, chopped
2 onions, chopped
1 cup yellow squash, chopped
3 teaspoons dried basil
Salt and pepper to taste
Coconut oil to grease, melted

Directions:
1. Grease a heatproof dish with coconut oil.
2. Add all the ingredients to the dish and stir. Cover the dish with foil.
3. Pour 1½ cups water into the Instant Pot. Place a trivet in the pot. Place the dish on the trivet.
4. Close the lid, press the MANUAL or PRESSURE COOK setting, and cook at high pressure for 20 minutes.
5. When the cooking is complete, do a natural pressure release.
6. Slice and serve warm.

Nutritional Information (Per Serving)
Calories: 416; Fat: 24.1g; Net Carbohydrates: 23.3g; Protein: 23.9 g

Almonds and Oats

Serves: 5
Preparation Time: 5 minutes
Cooking Time: 17 minutes
Ingredients:
1 cup steel-cut oats
2 cups coconut milk
1½ cups water
1 tablespoon butter
¼ cup sliced almonds
¼ cup chocolate chips
¼ teaspoon salt
1 teaspoon cinnamon
1 teaspoon nutmeg

Directions:
1. Set your Instant Pot to SAUTÉ and melt the butter in the pot.
2. Add the oats and toast for 2 minutes, stirring occasionally. You want them to smell toasty and begin to brown.
3. Add the coconut milk, water, salt, cinnamon, and nutmeg.
4. Close the lid, choose the MANUAL or PRESSURE COOK setting, and cook at high pressure for 10 minutes.
5. When the cooking is complete, do a natural pressure release for 10 minutes. Quick release the remaining pressure.
6. Carefully remove the lid and stir everything. Let it sit for 5 more minutes so the oats can thicken.
7. Add chocolate and almonds to the top and serve.

Nutritional Information (Per Serving)
Calories: 379; Fat: 31.3g; Net Carbohydrates: 18g; Protein: 6.1g

Instant Pot Apple Cranberry Oats

Serves: 6
Preparation Time: 5 minutes
Cooking Time: 11 minutes
Ingredients:
2 cups oats
2 tablespoons butter
2 cups whole milk
1 cup almond milk
3 cups water
3 large apples, peeled and diced
1½ cups cranberries
¼ teaspoon salt
½ teaspoon cinnamon
1 tablespoon lemon juice
2 teaspoons vanilla extract
¼ cup maple syrup

Directions:
1. In a bowl, soak the maple syrup with vanilla extract for about an hour.
2. Add the butter to the Instant Pot and set it to SAUTÉ. Add the oats and fry for about a minute.
3. Add the water, and whole milk, followed by almond milk, and give it a stir. Add the maple syrup mixture and stir again.
4. Sprinkle with the cinnamon powder and salt, and close the lid.
5. Choose the MANUAL or PRESSURE COOK setting, and cook at high pressure for 10 minutes.
6. When the cooking is complete, do a natural pressure release.
7. Open the lid, add the lemon juice and gently mix.
8. Garnish with diced apples and cranberries and serve.

Nutritional Information (Per Serving)
Calories: 383; Fat: 18.1g; Net Carbohydrates: 43.3g; Protein: 7.5g

Pumpkin Porridge

Serves: 4
Preparation Time: 5 minutes
Cooking Time: 12 minutes
Ingredients:
1 cup steel-cut oats
½ cup pumpkin puree
3 cups water
1 tablespoon butter
¼ teaspoon salt
1 teaspoon brown sugar
Dash of cinnamon (or nutmeg)

Directions:
1. Melt butter in the Instant Pot on SAUTÉ for 2 minutes.
2. Add the oats, pumpkin, water, salt, and sugar.
3. Close the lid securely and cook at high pressure for 10 minutes.
4. Wait another 10 minutes for the natural pressure to release.
5. Top the porridge with cinnamon or nutmeg and serve.

Nutritional Information (Per Serving)
Calories: 116; Fat: 4.3g; Net Carbohydrates: 14.1g; Protein: 3.1g

Gluten-Free and Vegan Buckwheat Porridge

Serves: 6
Preparation Time: 5 minutes
Cooking Time: 10 minutes
Ingredients:
1 cup buckwheat groats
3 cups coconut milk
1 large ripe banana, sliced
1 teaspoon cinnamon powder
1 teaspoon vanilla extract
¼ cup honey
¼ cup raisins
1 cup grated coconut
Some chopped walnuts

Directions:
1. Rinse the buckwheat with water and drain. Add all the ingredients except the walnuts to the Instant Pot. Mix well.
2. Close the lid, choose the MANUAL or PRESSURE COOK setting, and cook at high pressure for 10 minutes.
3. When the cooking is complete, do a natural pressure release.
4. Transfer the porridge into a large bowl.
5. Garnish with walnuts and serve.

Nutritional Information (Per Serving)
Calories: 474; Fat: 33.8g; Net Carbohydrates: 37.9g; Protein: 6.2g

Blueberry Bowl

Serves: 4
Preparation Time: 1 hour 10 minutes
Cooking Time: 1 minute
Ingredients:
1 tablespoon honey + extra for serving
1½ cups water
2 small cinnamon stick
1½ cups white quinoa
¼ cup raisins
1 cup apples, grated
1 cup apple juice
1 cup plain yogurt
¼ cup pistachios, chopped
6 tablespoons blueberries

Directions:
1. Rinse the quinoa and strain it through a fine mesh strainer.
2. Add the quinoa, water, and cinnamon stick to your Instant Pot, locking the lid. Cook at high pressure for 1 minute.
3. When cooking is complete, allow pressure to release naturally for 10 minutes. Quick release the remaining pressure.
4. Spoon the quinoa into a bowl and remove the cinnamon stick. Allow it to cool, then add the apple, apple juice, raisins, and honey. Stir to combine.
5. Refrigerate for at least 1 hour or overnight.
6. Add the yogurt, stirring well.
7. Serve topped with honey and blueberries.

Nutritional Information (Per Serving)
Calories: 416; Fat: 6.4g; Net Carbohydrates: 67.5g; Protein: 13.8g

Rice Pudding Parfait

Serves: 6
Preparation Time: 5 minutes
Cooking Time: 21 minutes
Ingredients:
1 cup white rice
1½ cups water
2 cups milk, divided
¼ cup sugar
2 eggs, beaten
½ teaspoon vanilla extract
1 cup raisins
¼ teaspoon salt
½ teaspoon cinnamon
½ cup blueberries

Directions:
1. Place the rice, water, and salt in the Instant Pot. Cook at high pressure for 3 minutes.
2. When the cooking is complete, do a natural pressure release for 10 minutes, then quick release the remaining pressure.
3. Open the lid, and add one cup of milk, the sugar, and cinnamon. Stir everything together.
4. In a separate bowl, mix the eggs with the other cup of milk. Add the mixture to the pressure cooker.
5. Set the Instant Pot to SAUTÉ and stir while cooking for 3 minutes, until the mixture starts to boil.
6. Press CANCEL, add the raisins, and leave the mixture to cool and thicken for 5 minutes. Top with blueberries.

Nutritional Information (Per Serving)
Calories: 286; Fat: 3.5g; Net Carbohydrates: 56.5g; Protein: 7.6g

Potato Bacon Gratin

Serves: 6
Preparation Time: 20 minutes
Cooking Time: 25 minutes
Ingredients:
6 medium potatoes, peeled and thinly sliced
6 strips of bacon, cooked and crumbled
1 cup heavy cream
1 cup grated cheddar cheese
2 garlic cloves, minced
½ cup onion, finely chopped
1 tablespoon olive oil
1 cup water
Salt and pepper to taste
½ cup grated Parmesan cheese
Chopped parsley, for garnish

Directions:
1. Slice the potatoes and keep them submerged in cold water to avoid discoloration.
2. Set the Instant Pot to SAUTÉ. Add the olive oil, garlic, and onion. Cook until the onion is translucent.
3. Add the bacon and give it a quick stir.
4. Drain the potatoes from the cold water and pat them dry. Layer half of the potato slices at the bottom of the Instant Pot.
5. Add one cup of water over the potatoes.
6. Sprinkle half of the cheddar cheese, salt, and pepper.
7. Add another layer of potatoes and repeat with the cheese and seasoning.
8. Pour the heavy cream over the layered potatoes.
9. Close the lid, choose the MANUAL or PRESSURE COOK setting, and cook at high pressure for 15 minutes.
10. When the cooking is complete, do a quick pressure release.
11. Sprinkle with the Parmesan cheese.
12. If you have an air fryer lid for your Instant Pot, you can use it to brown the top. Set it to 400°F and cook for about 10 minutes

or until the top is golden brown. You can also transfer the gratin to an oven-safe dish and broil in an oven for a few minutes until golden brown.

13. Sprinkle with chopped parsley and serve hot!

Nutritional Information (Per Serving)
Calories: 351; Fat: 21g; Net Carbohydrates: 27g; Protein: 12g

Egg Croissants

Serves: 4
Preparation Time: 10 minutes
Cooking Time: 8 minutes
Ingredients:
4 large eggs
Salt and pepper to taste
4 slices of cooked bacon, broken into small pieces
5 tablespoons shredded cheddar cheese
1 green scallion, diced
4 croissants

Directions:
1. Place a steamer basket inside the Instant Pot and pour in 1½ cups water.
2. Whip the eggs in a bowl. Add the bacon pieces, cheese, and scallion to the eggs. Mix well.
3. Divide the mixture into 4 muffin cups. Transfer the filled muffin cups onto the steamer basket.
4. Shut the lid and cook at high pressure for 8 minutes.
5. When the cooking is complete, wait a few minutes, and use a quick pressure release.
6. Lift the muffin cups out of the Instant Pot.
7. Slice 4 croissants in half and stuff with the muffin cup content.

Nutritional Information (Per Serving)
Calories: 482; Fat: 29.9g; Net Carbohydrates: 29.8g; Protein: 21g

Sausage and Bacon Frittata

Serves: 6
Preparation Time: 10 minutes
Cooking Time: 30 minutes
Ingredients:
8 large eggs
¼ cup milk
½ pound ground sausage
6 slices of bacon, chopped
½ cup bell pepper, diced
¼ cup onion, diced
½ cup grated cheddar cheese
¼ teaspoon salt
¼ teaspoon black pepper
1 cup water

Directions:
1. In a bowl, whisk together the eggs, milk, salt, and pepper. Transfer the egg mixture to a greased baking dish that will fit into your Instant Pot.
2. Set the Instant Pot to SAUTÉ. Add the bacon and cook until it starts to turn crispy, about 3–4 minutes. Add the ground sausage and continue cooking until browned, breaking up the sausage into smaller pieces.
3. Add the bell pepper and onion. Sauté for another 2–3 minutes, or until the onion becomes translucent.
4. Turn off the Instant Pot. Transfer the meat and vegetable mixture to the baking dish that contains the egg mixture. Sprinkle the cheese on top. Cover the dish with foil.
5. Clean the inner pot, then pour 1 cup of water into the pot. Place a trivet in the pot, and place the baking dish on the trivet.

6. Close the lid, choose the MANUAL or PRESSURE COOK setting, and cook at high pressure for 12 minutes.

7. When the cooking is complete, do a natural pressure release for 10 minutes. Quick release the remaining pressure.

8. Using oven mitts, carefully remove the dish with the frittata from the Instant Pot. Allow it to cool for a few minutes, then slice into wedges and serve.

Nutritional Information (Per Serving)
Calories: 275; Fat: 22g; Net Carbohydrates: 2g; Protein: 16g

French Toast

Serves: 6
Preparation Time: 10 minutes
Cooking Time: 20 minutes
Ingredients:
6 slices day-old French bread
4 bananas, peeled and sliced
3 large eggs
½ cup milk
3 tablespoons brown sugar
¼ cup cream cheese
2 tablespoons granulated sugar
1 teaspoon vanilla
½ teaspoon cinnamon
2 tablespoons sliced butter that is still hard
¼ cup chopped pecans

Directions:
1. Dice the bread into cubes.

2. Use a baking dish that will fit into the Instant Pot. Butter the inside of the dish.

3. Add half of the bread cubes to the dish. Top the bread cubes with 1 sliced banana and 1 tablespoon brown sugar.

4. Soften the cream cheese in a microwave. Spread the cream cheese over the bread cubes and banana layer
5. Add another layer of bread cubes, sliced banana, and brown sugar.
6. Place the chilled butter slices on top of the last lawyer.
7. In a bowl, whisk together the eggs, milk, sugar, vanilla, and cinnamon. Drench the bread with the egg mixture.
8. Fill the Instant Pot with a cup of water.
9. Place a trivet in the Instant Pot. Place the dish on the trivet.
10. Close the lid and cook at high pressure for 20 minutes.
11. When the cooking is complete, do a quick pressure release.
12. Open the lid and remove the French toast dish. Let sit for 5 minutes.
13. If desired, top the French toast with the remaining sliced banana, maple syrup, and pecans.

Nutritional Information (Per Serving)
Calories: 319; Fat: 11.9g; Net Carbohydrates: 43.2g; Protein: 9.4g

No-Crust Quiche

Serves: 4
Preparation Time: 10 minutes
Cooking Time: 30 minutes
Ingredients:
6 large beaten eggs
½ cup milk
Salt and pepper to taste
½ cup ham, diced
½ cup bacon, cooked and crumbled
2 scallions, chopped
1 cup shredded cheese

Directions:
1. Place a trivet inside the Instant Pot and fill it with 1½ cups of water.
2. In a bowl, beat together the eggs and milk; season with salt and pepper.
3. In a soufflé dish, combine the remaining ingredients.
4. Add the egg mixture to the soufflé dish and stir well. Cover the soufflé dish with foil.
5. Place the dish on the trivet.
6. Close the lid and cook at high pressure for 30 minutes.
7. When the cooking is complete, do a natural pressure release for 10 minutes. Quick release the remaining pressure.
8. Carefully lift out the dish and let it cool.
9. Lift off the foil and serve.
Note: For a browner quiche, add some additional cheese and place under the broiler for 5 minutes.

Nutritional Information (Per Serving)
Calories: 322; Fat: 24.2g; Net Carbohydrates: 3.9g; Protein: 22.3g

Instant Quinoa

Serves: 6
Preparation Time: 5 minutes
Cooking Time: 1 minute
Ingredients:
2 cups quinoa, rinsed
2½ cups water
2 tablespoons brown sugar
½ teaspoon vanilla extract
⅓ teaspoon cinnamon
Dash of salt

Directions:

1. Add all of the ingredients to the Instant Pot. Stir thoroughly to combine.

2. Cook for 1 minute at high pressure.

3. When the cooking is complete, do a natural pressure release for 10 minutes. Quick release the remaining pressure.

4. Open the lid carefully. Serve quinoa with milk, almond slivers, and berries.

Nutritional Information (Per Serving)
Calories: 221; Fat: 3.4g; Net Carbohydrates: 35.5g; Protein: 8.0g

Scrambled Eggs

Serves: 4
Preparation Time: 5 minutes
Cooking Time: 5 minutes
Ingredients:
8 large eggs
¼ cup milk
1 tablespoon butter
1 onion, chopped
Salt and pepper to taste

Directions:
1. In a bowl, beat the eggs with milk until well-combined. Season with salt and pepper.
2. Set your Instant Pot to SAUTÉ and melt the butter in the pot.
3. Add the onion, and sauté until onion is translucent.
4. Pour the egg mixture into the Instant Pot. Constantly stir the eggs to ensure even cooking.
5. Once the eggs are mostly cooked but still slightly runny, turn off the Instant Pot. Serve immediately.

Nutritional Information (Per Serving)
Calories: 183; Fat: 13g; Net Carbohydrates: 3g; Protein: 13g

Eggs in Bell Pepper Cups

Serves: 4
Preparation Time: 15 minutes
Cooking Time: 4 minutes
Ingredients:
4 bell peppers
4 eggs
Salt and pepper to taste
4 tablespoons mozzarella cheese, freshly grated

Directions:
1. With a sharp knife, cut the bell pepper ends to form about 1½-inch high cup. Remove the seeds completely.
2. Carefully, crack 1 egg in each bell pepper cup. Cover each bell pepper with a piece of foil.
3. In the bottom of the Instant Pot, arrange a steamer trivet and pour ½ cup of water.
4. Place the bell peppers on top of the trivet.
5. Close the lid, select the MANUAL or PRESSURE COOK setting, and cook at low pressure for 4 minutes.
6. When the cooking is complete, do a quick pressure release.
7. Open the lid and transfer the bell pepper cups onto serving plates.
8. Sprinkle with salt, pepper, and cheese and serve.

Nutritional Information (Per Serving)
Calories: 181; Fat: 9.7g; Net Carbohydrates: 8.8g; Protein: 14.7g

Veggie Hash

Serves: 3
Preparation Time: 15 minutes
Cooking Time: 8 minutes
Ingredients:
2 cups sweet potato, peeled and chopped
1 cup bell pepper, seeded and chopped
1 medium onion, chopped
1 garlic clove, minced
1 tablespoon olive oil
Salt and pepper to taste
1 teaspoon ground cumin
1 teaspoon paprika
Pinch of cayenne
½ cup water

Directions:
1. In the Instant Pot, mix all ingredients.
2. Close the lid, select the MANUAL or PRESSURE COOK setting, and cook at high pressure for 1 minute.
3. When the cooking is complete, do a natural pressure release.
4. Remove the lid and select SAUTÉ.
5. Cook for 6–8 minutes, stirring occasionally.
6. Serve hot.

Nutritional Information (Per Serving)
Calories: 194; Fat: 5.7g; Net Carbohydrates: 29g; Protein: 3.8g

CHAPTER THREE

Poultry

Chicken Teriyaki

Serves: 4
Preparation Time: 5 minutes
Cooking Time: 10 minutes
Ingredients:
1½ pounds boneless chicken breast, cut into 1-inch pieces
1 cup pineapple chunks
1 cup chicken stock
¼ cup brown sugar
1 tablespoon soy sauce
¼ cup apple cider vinegar
1 tablespoon ground ginger
1 tablespoon garlic powder
1 teaspoon black pepper
1 tablespoon cornstarch
1 tablespoon water

Directions:
1. In a bowl, combine the brown sugar, soy sauce, vinegar, ginger, garlic powder and pepper until the sugar dissolves.
2. Place the chicken breasts in the Instant Pot and top with pineapple and chicken stock.
3. Pour the sugar mixture on top of that. Stir carefully to coat the chicken.
4. Close the lid, select the MANUAL or PRESSURE COOK setting, and cook high pressure for 10 minutes.
5. When the cooking is complete, do a natural pressure release.
6. Remove the chicken from the pot but keep the liquid.
7. In a small bowl, mix the cornstarch and water until smooth.

8. Set the Instant Pot to SAUTÉ and, once the liquid begins to simmer, stir in the cornstarch mixture. Continue to stir until the liquid thickens. Use as a teriyaki sauce over the chicken.

Nutritional Information (Per Serving)
Calories: 275; Fat: 4.5g; Net Carbohydrates: 18.4g; Protein: 36.8g

Pesto Chicken

Serves: 4
Preparation Time: 10 minutes
Cooking Time: 15 minutes
Ingredients:
4 boneless, skinless chicken breasts
1 cup basil pesto
½ cup water
½ cup grated Parmesan cheese
1 cup cherry tomatoes, halved
½ teaspoon salt
¼ teaspoon black pepper
2 tablespoons olive oil
Fresh basil leaves for garnish

Directions:
1. Season the chicken breasts on both sides with salt and pepper.
2. Set your Instant Pot to SAUTÉ and add the olive oil.
3. Place the chicken breasts in the pot and sear for 2–3 minutes on each side, or until browned. Remove the chicken and set aside.
4. Pour ½ cup water into the pot, scraping up any browned bits from the bottom using a wooden spoon.
5. Place the seared chicken breasts back into the pot.
6. Spread the pesto sauce evenly over each chicken breast.
7. Sprinkle Parmesan cheese over the chicken.
8. Scatter the cherry tomatoes around and on top of the chicken.

9. Close the lid, select the MANUAL or PRESSURE COOK setting, and cook at high pressure for 10 minutes.

10. When the cooking is complete, do a natural pressure release for 10 minutes. Quick release the remaining pressure.

11. Garnish with fresh basil leaves and serve.

Nutritional Information (Per Serving)
Calories: 518; Fat: 39g; Net Carbohydrates: 4g; Protein: 38g

Lemon Coconut Chicken

Serves: 6
Preparation Time: 5 minutes
Cooking Time: 20 minutes
Ingredients:
1 cup coconut milk
¼ cup lemon juice
Some lemon zest
1 teaspoon turmeric powder
1 tablespoon curry powder
1 cup broccoli florets
4 pounds chicken thighs and breasts, cubed
1 teaspoon salt

Directions:
1. Roast the broccoli florets in a pan for 3–4 minutes.

2. In an Instant Pot, add the coconut milk, lemon juice, turmeric powder, curry powder, and salt and mix well.

3. Slide in the chicken pieces. Sprinkle in lemon juice and stir again. Cover the lid of the pot and cook for 15 minutes at high pressure.

4. When the cooking is complete, do a natural pressure release.

5. Remove the chicken, and place in a large bowl.

6. Sprinkle some lemon zest on top and add the broccoli florets.

7. Serve hot.

Nutritional Information (Per Serving)
Calories: 449; Fat: 17.4g; Net Carbohydrates: 2.6g; Protein: 65.7g

Duck in Lemon Sauce

Serves: 4
Preparation Time: 20 minutes
Cooking Time: 30 minutes
Ingredients:
1 pound duck breast, cubed
1 tablespoon olive oil
2 cups chicken broth
Zest and juice of 2 large lemons
4 garlic cloves, minced
1 tablespoon fresh ginger, minced
1 tablespoon honey
1 tablespoon soy sauce
1 tablespoon cornstarch mixed with 2 tablespoons of cold water (slurry)
Salt and pepper to taste
Fresh parsley, finely chopped for garnish

Directions:
1. Season the duck with salt and pepper. Prepare the cornstarch slurry by mixing it with cold water.
2. Set your Instant Pot to SAUTÉ and add the olive oil.
3. Add the duck pieces, skin-side down. Brown for about 4–5 minutes on each side. Remove the duck pieces and set aside.
4. Add the garlic and ginger to the pot and sauté for 1 minute. Stir in the lemon zest, lemon juice, honey, and soy sauce. Mix well.
5. Return the browned duck pieces to the pot. Pour in the chicken broth.
6. Close the lid, select the MANUAL or PRESSURE COOK setting, and cook at high pressure for 5 minutes.

7. When the cooking is complete, do a natural pressure release for 10 minutes. Quick release the remaining pressure.
8. Remove the duck pieces from the pot and set aside.
9. Set the Instant Pot to SAUTÉ and stir in the cornstarch slurry to thicken the sauce. Allow the sauce to boil for 2–3 minutes.
10. Pour the lemon sauce over the duck pieces.
11. Garnish with fresh parsley and serve.

Nutritional Information (Per Serving)
Calories: 271; Fat: 14g; Net Carbohydrates: 9g; Protein: 25g

Pina Colada Chicken

Serves: 4
Preparation Time: 10 minutes
Cooking Time: 20 minutes
Ingredients:
2 pounds chicken thighs, cut into small pieces
1 cup pineapple, diced
½ cup coconut cream
½ teaspoon salt
1 teaspoon ground cinnamon
¾ cup green onion, chopped
2 tablespoons desiccated coconut shavings
1 tablespoon arrowroot powder
1 tablespoon water

Directions:
1. Add all the above ingredients to an Instant Pot except for the green onions and mix well.
2. Press the POULTRY button and cook for 15 minutes at high pressure.
3. Do a quick pressure release.

4. Add the arrowroot powder to a tablespoon of water, mix, and add it to the chicken. Let it simmer for a few minutes until it thickens.

5. Garnish with chopped green onions and serve.

Nutritional Information (Per Serving)
Calories: 572; Fat: 26.1g; Net Carbohydrates: 11.4g; Protein: 66.9g

Chili Chicken

Serves: 6
Preparation Time: 10 minutes
Cooking Time: 20 minutes
Ingredients:
2 tablespoons olive oil
3 chicken breasts, cubed
1 cup onion, chopped
2 garlic cloves, minced
1 cup bell pepper, chopped
1 cup chicken broth
2 cups tomatoes, diced
1 can (15 ounces) chili beans
½ cup Picante sauce
½ teaspoon salt
1 teaspoon chili powder

Directions:
1. Set your Instant Pot to SAUTÉ.
2. Heat the olive oil, add chicken, and sauté until browned.
3. Add the onion, pepper, garlic and cook for 4 minutes.
4. Add the rest of the ingredients.
5. Close the lid, choose the MANUAL or PRESSURE COOK setting, and cook at high pressure for 10 minutes.
6. When the cooking is complete, do a natural pressure release.
7. Serve over rice.

Nutritional Information (Per Serving)
Calories: 478; Fat: 16.1g; Net Carbohydrates: 11g; Protein: 65.5g

Barbecue Chicken

Serves: 4
Preparation Time: 5 minutes
Cooking Time: 15 minutes
Ingredients:
2 chicken breasts, split in half
1 cup chicken stock
½ cup water
1 teaspoon nutmeg
1 teaspoon cinnamon
1 teaspoon ginger
¼ teaspoon salt
1 teaspoon pepper
½ cup barbecue sauce (use your favorite)

Directions:
1. Combine the salt, pepper, ginger, cinnamon, and nutmeg in a small bowl and rub the mixture into the chicken breasts.
2. Place them in the Instant Pot and cover with the water and the chicken stock.
3. Set the Instant Pot at high pressure and cook for 15 minutes.
4. When the cooking is complete, use a natural pressure release.
5. Remove the chicken and cover with barbecue sauce.

Nutritional Information (Per Serving)
Calories: 128; Fat: 1.9g; Net Carbohydrates: 12.1g; Protein: 14.1g

Cacciatore Chicken

Serves: 4
Preparation Time: 10 minutes
Cooking Time: 20 minutes
Ingredients:
6 chicken thighs
1 large yellow onion, chopped
1 cup chicken broth
1 bay leaf
1 teaspoon garlic powder
1 teaspoon oregano
¾ cup black olives
¼ teaspoon salt
6 medium tomatoes, chopped

Directions:
1. Heat the Instant Pot by setting it on SAUTÉ.
2. Slide the chicken thighs into the pot. Add chopped onion, bay leaf, chicken broth, garlic powder, oregano, salt, and tomatoes and mix well. Close the lid and cook at high pressure for 15 minutes.
3. When the cooking is complete, do a natural pressure release.
4. Transfer the mixture to a large plate.
5. Garnish with some olives and serve.

Nutritional Information (Per Serving)
Calories: 327; Fat: 18.5g; Net Carbohydrates: 9.1g; Protein: 27.3g

Sweet Garlic Chicken

Serves: 6
Preparation Time: 10 minutes
Cooking Time: 10 minutes
Ingredients:
3 pounds chicken drumsticks and thighs
2 cloves garlic, minced
2 teaspoons garlic Sriracha chili sauce
2 tablespoons soy sauce
½ cup ketchup
½ cup honey
2 tablespoons brown sugar
2 tablespoons fresh basil, chopped
Salt and pepper to taste
1 tablespoon cornstarch
1 tablespoon water

Directions:
1. In a bowl, whisk together the garlic, chili sauce, soy sauce, ketchup, honey, and brown sugar until the sugar dissolves.
2. Pour the mixture into the Instant Pot.
3. Season the chicken pieces with salt and pepper, and place them into the pot.
4. Cook at high pressure for about 10 minutes.
5. When the cooking is complete, do a natural pressure release.
6. Take the chicken out of the pot but keep the liquid.
6. Stir in the cornstarch and the water, allowing the sauce to thicken. Pour it on top of the chicken before you serve.

Nutritional Information (Per Serving)
Calories: 388; Fat: 5.8g; Net Carbohydrates: 33.7g; Protein: 49.1g

Cajun Chicken with Rice

Serves: 4
Preparation Time: 10 minutes
Cooking Time: 15 minutes
Ingredients:
1 pound chicken breast, cubed
1 tablespoon Cajun seasoning
1 tablespoon olive oil
1 onion, diced
2 garlic cloves, minced
1 tablespoon tomato paste
1½ cups white rice, rinsed
2 red bell peppers, diced
2 cups vegetable broth

Directions:
1. Place the oil in the Instant Pot and select SAUTÉ. Add garlic and onion. Cook until browned, stirring frequently.
2. Press CANCEL, and add chicken breast, tomato paste, rice, Cajun seasoning, bell pepper, and vegetable broth. Stir well to combine.
3. Close the lid and cook at high pressure for 10 minutes.
4. When the cooking is complete, do a natural pressure release for 10 minutes. Quick release the remaining pressure.
5. Stir to combine before serving.

Nutritional Information (Per Serving)
Calories: 470; Fat: 7.7g; Net Carbohydrates: 62.4g; Protein: 32.7g

Chicken Thighs with Feta Cheese

Serves: 4
Preparation Time: 15 minutes
Cooking Time: 20 minutes
Ingredients:
4 bone-in, skin-on chicken thighs
¾ cup crumbled feta cheese
½ cup chicken broth
1 small red onion, thinly sliced
3 garlic cloves, minced
1 cup cherry tomatoes, halved
2 tablespoons olive oil
1 teaspoon dried oregano
Salt and pepper to taste
Fresh parsley, finely chopped for garnish

Directions:
1. Season the chicken thighs on both sides with salt, pepper, and dried oregano.
2. Set your Instant Pot to SAUTÉ and add the olive oil.
3. Add the chicken thighs, skin-side down, and sear for 4–5 minutes or until the skin is golden. Flip and sear the other side for 3 minutes. Remove the chicken thighs and set aside.
4. In the pot, add the red onion and sauté for 2–3 minutes or until softened.
5. Add the garlic and cook for 30 seconds until fragrant.
6. Pour in the chicken broth, scraping the bottom to loosen any browned bits.
7. Return the seared chicken thighs, skin-side up, to the pot.
8. Scatter the cherry tomatoes around the chicken.
9. Close the lid, select the MANUAL or PRESSURE COOK setting, and cook at high pressure for 15 minutes.
10. When the cooking is complete, do a natural pressure release for 10 minutes. Quick release the remaining pressure.
11. Carefully open the lid. Sprinkle the feta cheese over the chicken thighs.

12. Close the lid and let the residual heat melt the cheese for about 2 minutes.

13. Garnish with fresh parsley and serve.

Nutritional Information (Per Serving)
Calories: 420; Fat: 34g; Net Carbohydrates: 4g; Protein: 23g

Chicken Salad

Serves: 8
Preparation Time: 15 minutes
Cooking Time: 8 minutes
Ingredients:
For chicken:
15 ounces tomatoes, diced
½ cup onion, diced
3 garlic cloves, minced
2 tablespoons tomato paste
Salt and pepper to taste
¼ teaspoon coriander
¼ teaspoon cocoa powder
1 teaspoon cumin
1 teaspoon chili powder
2 pounds chicken meat

For Salad:
10 cups torn romaine lettuce
1 cup cilantro, chopped
4 scallions, chopped
2 cups cherry tomatoes, sliced in half
2 cups cubed cheddar cheese
½ cup olives, chopped
2 avocados, diced
Ranch dressing

Directions:
1. Stir all taco ingredients, except the chicken, into an Instant Pot.
2. Place the chicken on top of the ingredients. Cook at high pressure for 8 minutes.
3. Allow pressure to release naturally.
4. Transfer the chicken to a platter and shred the meat.
5. Place the sauce in a blender and puree for smoothness.
6. Combine all salad ingredients in a bowl. Top with the chicken.
7. Drizzle the sauce over the salad.
8. Serve with ranch dressing.

Nutritional Information (Per Serving)
Calories: 473; Fat: 28.9g; Net Carbohydrates: 6.6g; Protein: 42.2g

Turkey Meatballs

Serves: 6
Preparation Time: 10 minutes
Cooking Time: 8 minutes
Ingredients:
1½ pounds ground turkey breast
1 cup breadcrumbs
1 onion, diced
2 cloves garlic, minced
¼ cup milk
1 teaspoon dried Italian seasoning
1 egg
2 tablespoons ketchup
1 can whole tomatoes
1 cup water

Directions:
1. Make the meatballs by combining the turkey breast, breadcrumbs, onion, garlic, milk, seasoning, egg, and ketchup.
2. Use your hands to combine all those ingredients and form small balls.
3. Pour the whole tomatoes, with their juices, into the Instant Pot and add water. Mix the liquids.
4. Add the meatballs. Cook at high pressure for 8 minutes.
5. When the cooking is complete, do a natural pressure release.
6. Remove the meatballs and cover them with the sauce.

Nutritional Information (Per Serving)
Calories: 218; Fat: 3.2g; Net Carbohydrates: 16.6g; Protein: 29.2g

Simple Herb Turkey Breast

Serves: 6
Preparation Time: 10 minutes
Cooking Time: 20 minutes
Ingredients:
3 pounds turkey breast
2 cups chicken broth
1 red onion, quartered
3 stalks celery, roughly chopped
1 sprig fresh thyme
2 sprigs fresh rosemary
1 teaspoon dried basil
1 teaspoon dried oregano
Salt and pepper

Directions:
1. Season turkey breasts with salt, pepper, dried basil, and dried oregano.
2. Place a trivet at the bottom of the Instant Pot and pour in the chicken broth.
3. Add the rosemary and thyme.
4. Place the turkey on top, breast side up. Add the onion and celery.
5. Cook at high pressure for 20 minutes.
6. When the cooking is complete, do a natural pressure release.
7. Serve with the sauce.

Nutritional Information (Per Serving)
Calories: 408; Fat: 11.9g; Net Carbohydrates: 1.8g; Protein: 68.3g

Turkey Goulash

Serves: 4
Preparation Time: 10 minutes
Cooking Time: 15 minutes
Ingredients:
2 pounds ground turkey breast
1 15-ounce can diced tomatoes
2 cloves garlic, chopped
1 red onion, sliced
1 red bell pepper, chopped
1 green bell pepper, chopped
1 cup chicken stock
1 tablespoon butter

Directions:
1. Heat the butter in the Instant Pot and set it to SAUTÉ. Add the ground turkey, cooking it for 5 minutes.
2. Add the tomatoes with their juices, the garlic, onion, peppers, and chicken stock.
3. Close the lid, select the MANUAL or PRESSURE COOK setting, and cook at high pressure for 15 minutes.
4. When the cooking is complete, do a quick pressure release.

Nutritional Information (Per Serving)
Calories: 508; Fat: 20.2g; Net Carbohydrates: 9.2g; Protein: 67.3g

Turkey in Orange-Ginger Sauce

Serves: 6
Preparation Time: 15 minutes
Cooking Time: 30 minutes
Ingredients:
2 pounds turkey breast, boneless and skinless
2 tablespoons olive oil
Salt and pepper to taste
3 cloves garlic, minced
2-inch piece of fresh ginger, grated
Zest and juice of 2 large oranges
¼ cup low-sodium soy sauce
1 tablespoon honey
½ cup chicken broth
2 tablespoons cornstarch
2 tablespoons water

Directions:
1. Season the turkey with salt and pepper on both sides.
2. Set your Instant Pot to SAUTÉ and add the olive oil.
3. Place the turkey pieces in the pot and sear for 2–3 minutes on each side. Transfer to a plate and set aside.
4. In the pot, add the garlic and ginger. Sauté for about 1 minute until fragrant.
5. Stir in the orange zest, orange juice, soy sauce, honey, and chicken broth. Mix well.
6. Place the turkey back into the Instant Pot, ensuring it's submerged in the sauce.
7. Set the Instant Pot at high pressure and cook for 20 minutes.
8. When the cooking is complete, do a natural pressure release for 10 minutes. Quick release the remaining pressure.
9. Remove the turkey from the pot and set aside.
10. In a small bowl, mix the cornstarch and water until smooth.
11. Set your Instant Pot to SAUTÉ and, once the sauce begins to simmer, stir in the cornstarch mixture. Continue to stir until the sauce thickens.

12. Return the turkey to the pot, coating it with the sauce. Simmer for 2–3 minutes.

13. Serve with steamed rice or roasted vegetables.

Nutritional Information (Per Serving)
Calories: 218; Fat: 6g; Net Carbohydrates: 8g; Protein: 31g

Roasted Cornish Hen

Serves: 4
Preparation Time: 10 minutes
Cooking Time: 19 minutes
Ingredients:
2 Cornish hens
Salt and pepper to taste
2 tablespoons olive oil
1 medium onion, chopped
2 celery stalks, chopped
2 medium carrots, peeled and chopped
4 garlic cloves, chopped
2 teaspoons Worcestershire sauce
1½ cups water

Directions:
1. Wash the hen and then with paper towels, pat it dry.

2. Rub salt and pepper over hen liberally.

3. Place the oil in the Instant Pot and select SAUTÉ. Add the hen and cook for 2 minutes per side.

4. Press CANCEL and top with remaining ingredients.

5. Secure the lid and cook at high pressure for 15 minutes.

6. When the cooking is complete, use a natural pressure release.

7. Transfer the hen onto a platter to cool for 5 minutes before serving.

8. Serve alongside the vegetables.

Nutritional Information (Per Serving)
Calories: 267; Fat: 12g; Net Carbohydrates: 6.3g; Protein: 30.8g

Buffalo Chicken

Serves: 6
Preparation Time: 10 minutes
Cooking Time: 45 minutes
Ingredients:
2 pounds chicken breast, cubed
2 tablespoons coconut oil
2 onions, chopped
1 cup homemade chicken broth
1 pound sweet potatoes, peeled and cubed
6 tablespoons buffalo sauce
1 teaspoon garlic powder
1 teaspoon onion powder
Salt and pepper to taste

Directions:
1. Select SAUTÉ and add the oil. When the oil is heated, add onions and sauté until brown.
2. Add the chicken, broth, sweet potatoes, buffalo sauce, salt, and all the spices into the pot. Mix well.
3. Close the lid, select the MANUAL or PRESSURE COOK setting, and cook at high pressure for 15 minutes.
4. When the cooking is complete, do a quick pressure release.

Nutritional Information (Per Serving)
Calories: 333; Fat: 8.7g; Net Carbohydrates: 22g; Protein: 34.5g

BBQ Chicken Thighs

Serves: 4
Preparation Time: 15 minutes
Cooking Time: 15 minutes
Ingredients:
2 tablespoons olive oil
1 onion, chopped
1 pound chicken thighs
1 garlic clove, minced
2 tablespoons tomato paste
1 tablespoon soy sauce
1 cup plus 2 tablespoons water
1½ tablespoons arrowroot
¼ teaspoon salt
¼ teaspoon pepper

Directions:
1. Heat the oil in your Instant Pot on SAUTÉ. Sauté the onions for a couple of minutes.
2. Add garlic and cook for 30–60 seconds, until fragrant.
3. Whisk in 1 cup of water with the tomato paste and soy sauce. Add the chicken thighs.
4. Close the lid, select the MANUAL or PRESSURE COOK setting, and cook at high pressure for 10 minutes.
5. Do a quick pressure release and transfer the thighs to a plate.
6. Add the remaining ingredients to the Instant Pot and whisk to combine.
7. Cook on SAUTÉ until the sauce thickens.
8. Return the chicken to the pot and coat well.
9. Serve hot.

Nutritional Information (Per Serving)
Calories: 323; Fat: 24.1g; Net Carbohydrates: 4.1g; Protein: 21.1g

Chicken and Broccoli

Serves: 4 servings
Preparation Time: 15 minutes
Cooking Time: 23 minutes
Ingredients:
1 tablespoon olive oil
2 (4-ounce) skinless, boneless chicken breasts
Salt and pepper to taste
1 small yellow onion, chopped
1 garlic clove, minced
1¼ cups chicken broth
1½ tablespoons arrowroot starch
3½ tablespoons water, divided
½ cup Cheddar cheese, shredded
2 ounces cream cheese, cubed
2 cups small broccoli florets

Directions:
1. Place the oil in the Instant Pot and select SAUTÉ. Add the chicken breasts and cook for 4–5 minutes.
2. With a slotted spoon, transfer the chicken breasts to a plate.
3. In the pot, add onion and cook for 2–3 minutes.
4. Add garlic and cook for about 1 minute.
5. Press CANCEL and stir in the cooked chicken and chicken broth.
6. Close the lid, select the MANUAL or PRESSURE COOK setting, and cook at high pressure for 5 minutes.
7. When the cooking is complete, do a quick pressure release.
8. Open the lid and with tongs, transfer chicken breasts onto a cutting board.
9. With a sharp knife, cut chicken into desired-sized pieces.
10. Meanwhile, in a small bowl, dissolve arrowroot starch in 1½ tablespoons of water.
11. Set the Instant Pot to SAUTÉ and add the arrowroot mixture, stirring continuously.

12. Add Cheddar cheese and cream cheese and cook until melted completely, stirring continuously.

13. Meanwhile, in a large microwave-safe bowl, add broccoli and 2 tablespoons of water and microwave on High for 3–4 minutes.

14. Add chopped chicken and broccoli to the Instant Pot and stir well. Simmer for 4–5 minutes.

15. Serve hot.

Nutritional Information (Per Serving)
Calories: 253; Fat: 15.7g; Net Carbohydrates: 6.7g; Protein: 20.3g

CHAPTER FOUR

Meats

Beef and Beans

Serves: 6
Preparation Time: 10 minutes
Cooking Time: 28 minutes
Ingredients:
1½ pounds stew meat
1 tablespoon olive oil
1 onion, chopped
2 garlic cloves, minced
2 cups beef broth
1 cup tomatoes, diced
1 tablespoon mustard
1 tablespoon taco seasoning
1 can (15 ounces) Kidney beans
1 can (15 ounces) chili beans
Salt and pepper to taste

Directions:
1. Set the Instant Pot to SAUTÉ.
2. Heat the olive oil and add stew meat. Sauté the meat until browned.
3. Add the onion and cook for 2 minutes. Add the garlic and cook for 1 more minute.
4. Pour in the broth, and add the rest of the ingredients.
5. Close the lid, set the Instant Pot to the MANUAL or PRESSURE COOK setting, and cook at high pressure for 20 minutes.
6. When the cooking is complete, do a natural pressure release.
7. Adjust the seasoning and serve over rice.

Nutritional Information (Per Serving)
Calories: 501; Fat: 22.5g; Net Carbohydrates: 19.1g; Protein: 46.4g

Beef Chili with Kale

Serves: 6
Preparation Time: 20 minutes
Cooking Time: 30 minutes
Ingredients:
2 pounds ground beef
1 large onion, chopped
3 garlic cloves, minced
2 large bell peppers (red or green), chopped
1 can (14 ounces) diced tomatoes, undrained
2 cans (15 ounces each) black beans, drained and rinsed
3 cups fresh kale, stems removed and chopped
3 tablespoons chili powder
1 tablespoon ground cumin
1 teaspoon oregano
Salt and pepper to taste
2 cups beef broth
1 tablespoon olive oil

Directions:
1. Set your Instant Pot to SAUTÉ and add the olive oil.
2. Add the onion and sauté until it becomes translucent.
3. Add the minced garlic and sauté for 1–2 minutes.
4. Add the ground beef, breaking it up with a spatula. Cook until browned.
5. Stir in the remaining ingredients, except for the kale.
6. Set the Instant Pot to the MANUAL or PRESSURE COOK setting and cook at high pressure for 20 minutes.
7. When the cooking is complete, do a natural pressure release for 10 minutes. Quick release the remaining pressure.

8. Open the lid carefully. Stir in the kale, and close the lid, allowing the kale to wilt from the residual heat.

9. Serve with your choice of toppings.

Nutritional Information (Per Serving)
Calories: 437; Fat: 23g; Net Carbohydrates: 21g; Protein: 33g

Beef Bourguignon

Serves: 4
Preparation Time: 10 minutes
Cooking Time: 50 minutes
Ingredients:
1 pound beef stew meat
4 bacon slices
2 garlic cloves, minced
2 medium onions, chopped
4 medium carrots, chopped
2 tablespoons parsley
2 tablespoons thyme
½ cup beef stock
1 cup red wine
2 large potatoes, cubed
1 tablespoon honey
1 tablespoon olive oil

Directions:
1. Place the oil in the Instant Pot and select SAUTÉ. Add beef and cook for 3–4 minutes or until browned. Set the beef aside.
2. Add bacon and onion, and sauté until onion is translucent.
3. Add beef and the rest of the ingredients and close the lid.
4. Cook at high pressure for 30 minutes.
5. When the cooking is complete, do a natural pressure release.
6. Serve warm.

Nutritional Information (Per Serving)
Calories: 559; Fat: 17g; Carbohydrates: 39.8g; Protein: 43.3g

Paleo Meatloaf

Serves: 4
Preparation Time: 15 minutes
Cooking Time: 30 minutes
Ingredients:
2 pounds ground beef
1 cup salsa
1 teaspoon cumin
½ teaspoon salt
1 teaspoon paprika
1 teaspoon chili powder
1 teaspoon garlic powder
1 teaspoon ground pepper
1 onion, diced
1 tablespoon tapioca flour
1 tablespoon olive oil
1½ cups water

Directions:
1. Pour the water into your Instant Pot and lower a trivet.
2. Grease a loaf pan that fits inside your Instant Pot with the olive oil.
3. Place the remaining ingredients in a large bowl. Mix with your hands until well incorporated. Transfer the mixture to the loaf pan and press firmly.
4. Place the loaf pan on the trivet and close the lid.
5. Set the Instant Pot to the MANUAL or PRESSURE COOK setting and cook at high pressure for 30 minutes.
6. Let the pressure release naturally for 10 minutes. Quick release the remaining pressure.
7. Slowly remove the meat. Serve hot.

Nutritional Information (Per Serving)
Calories: 491; Fat: 18.1g; Net Carbohydrates: 6.5g; Protein: 70.5g

Pork Chops with Tomatoes

Serves: 4
Preparation Time: 15 minutes
Cooking Time: 25 minutes
Ingredients:
4 bone-in pork chops
1 can (14 ounces) diced tomatoes with juice
1 medium-sized onion, thinly sliced
3 garlic cloves, minced
1 cup chicken broth
2 tablespoons olive oil
1 teaspoon dried basil
1 teaspoon dried oregano
Salt and pepper to taste

Directions:
1. Season both sides of each pork chop with salt and pepper. Set aside.
2. Set your Instant Pot to SAUTÉ and add the olive oil.
3. Add pork chops (in batches if necessary) and sear on each side for 2–3 minutes until browned. Remove and set aside.
4. Add the onion and sauté until it becomes translucent. Add the garlic and sauté for another minute.
5. Place the pork chops back into the Instant Pot. Pour the diced tomatoes (with juice) over the pork chops.
6. Sprinkle the dried basil and oregano over the mixture. Pour the chicken broth into the pot.
7. Close the lid, select the MANUAL or PRESSURE COOK setting, and cook at high pressure for 15 minutes.
8. When the cooking is complete, do a natural pressure release for 10 minutes. Quick release the remaining pressure.
9. Serve warm.

Nutritional Information (Per Serving)
Calories: 394; Fat: 25g; Net Carbohydrates: 6g; Protein: 30g

Sesame Beef & Broccoli

Serves: 4
Preparation Time: 10 minutes
Cooking Time: 20 minutes
Ingredients:
1 pound beef roast, sliced
2 tablespoons sesame oil
1 onion, chopped
3 cloves garlic, minced
1 cup beef broth
½ cup soy sauce
⅓ cup brown sugar
½ teaspoon red pepper flakes
1 pound broccoli
¼ cup peanuts
2 tablespoons sesame seeds
Salt and pepper to taste

Directions:
1. Set the Instant Pot to SAUTÉ. Coat the beef with sesame oil and season with salt and pepper, then place in the Instant Pot to brown.
2. Add onion and garlic and sauté for 2 minutes.
3. Add broth, brown sugar, soy sauce, red pepper flakes. Cook another 2 minutes.
4. Cover the pot and cook at high pressure for 10 minutes.
5. When the cooking is complete, do a natural pressure release.
6. Steam the broccoli while the beef cooks, in the microwave or stovetop.
7. Toss it all together.

Nutritional Information (Per Serving)
Calories: 474; Fat: 21.4g; Net Carbohydrates: 22.8g; Protein: 44.4g

Swedish Meatballs

Serves: 6
Preparation Time: 15 minutes
Cooking Time: 35 minutes
Ingredients:
1 pound ground beef
1 pound ground pork
6 tablespoons chopped parsley
2 teaspoons onion powder
1 teaspoon sage
¼ teaspoon allspice
Salt and pepper to taste
1 large diced onion
1½ cups sliced mushrooms
1 cup beef broth

Directions:

1. Use a bowl to combine the beef, pork, half the parsley, onion powder, sage, allspice, salt, and pepper. Form 1-inch meatballs.
2. Place the onion, mushrooms, and liquid into the Instant Pot.
3. Transfer the meatballs to the Instant Pot.
4. Lock the lid, Press MEAT, and cook for 35 minutes.
5. Use the quick release method to release pressure. Transfer the meatballs to a platter with a slotted spoon.
6. Pour the sauce into a blender and puree it into a smooth gravy.
7. Spoon the gravy over the meatballs and garnish with remaining parsley.
8. Serve over noodles or rice.

Nutritional Information (Per Serving)
Calories: 273; Fat: 7.7g; Net Carbohydrates: 3.1g; Protein: 44.6g

Maple Smoked Brisket

Serves: 4
Preparation Time: 5 minutes
Cooking Time: 55 minutes
Ingredients:
1½ pounds beef brisket
2 tablespoons brown sugar
1 teaspoon sea salt
1 teaspoon ground pepper
1 teaspoon mustard powder
1 tablespoon onion powder
½ teaspoon garlic powder
½ teaspoon paprika powder
1 tablespoon olive oil
2 cups chicken broth
1 tablespoon liquid smoke
Some fresh thyme leaves

Directions:
1. If the brisket is refrigerated, ensure you take it out and let it sit at room temperature for about 30 minutes.
2. In a bowl, combine brown sugar, sea salt, ground pepper, mustard powder, onion powder, garlic powder, and paprika powder.
3. Lay the brisket on a tray. Generously coat the meat with the above mixture.
4. Grease the bottom of the Instant Pot with olive oil. Heat for about 3 minutes on the SAUTÉ setting.
5. Transfer the brisket to the pot and cook on both sides until golden brown. Make sure you don't burn the brisket while doing this.
6. Pour the chicken broth on top of the brisket, followed by liquid smoke. Close the lid, select the MANUAL or PRESSURE COOK setting, and cook at high pressure for 50 minutes.
7. Serve with some thyme leaves on top.

Nutritional Information (Per Serving)

Calories: 395; Fat: 15.1g; Net Carbohydrates: 6.8g; Protein: 54.5g

Knorr Demi-Glace Brisket

Serves: 4
Preparation Time: 10 minutes
Cooking Time: 70 minutes
Ingredients:
2 tablespoons olive oil
2 pounds beef brisket
1 onion, chopped
2 celery stalks, chopped
2 garlic cloves, minced
2 bay leaves
1¼ cups beef broth
2 tablespoons Knorr Demi-glace sauce
1 tablespoon Worcestershire sauce
½ teaspoon salt
½ teaspoon black pepper

Directions:
1. Season the brisket with salt and pepper.
2. Heat 1 tablespoon of olive oil in your Instant Pot on SAUTÉ and add the beef. Sear for about 2 minutes per side. Transfer to a plate.
3. Heat the other tablespoon of oil and add the onion and celery. Cook until soft. Stir in the garlic and cook for another minute.
4. Return the beef to the pot and add the bay leaves.
5. In a bowl, whisk together the broth and sauces and pour the mixture over the beef.
6. Close the lid, select MEAT/STEW, and cook for 1 hour.
7. When the cooking is complete, use a natural pressure release.
8. Serve and enjoy!

Nutritional Information (Per Serving)

Calories: 735; Fat: 58.3g; Net Carbohydrates: 6.1g; Protein: 45.8g

Mongolian Beef

Serves: 6
Preparation Time: 10 minutes
Cooking Time: 25 minutes
Ingredients:
2 pounds steak, sliced
1 tablespoon coconut oil
4 garlic cloves, minced
3 medium-sized white onions, finely chopped
1 teaspoon minced ginger
3 tablespoons dark soy sauce
½ cup water
3 tablespoons brown sugar
2 tablespoons corn flour
Salt and pepper to taste
Some chives

Directions:
1. Lay the steak on a tray. Season it with salt and pepper from all sides.
2. Grease the Instant Pot with coconut oil and set it to SAUTÉ. As the oil starts sizzling, transfer the steak in batches. Once browned on both sides, set it aside.
3. Add some coconut oil to the Instant Pot. Throw in the minced garlic, ginger, and chopped onions and sauté for 2–3 minutes. Add soy sauce and water and give it a stir.
4. Transfer the browned beef to the pot, close the lid, and cook at high pressure for 15 minutes.
5. When the cooking is complete, press CANCEL, and do a natural pressure release.

6. Combine the cornstarch with water in a bowl and whisk. Pour this mixture into the pot, stirring continuously. Set the Instant Pot to SAUTÉ. Bring it to a boil until it thickens.

7. Serve with some chopped chives on top.

Nutritional Information (Per Serving)
Calories: 377; Fat: 10g; Net Carbohydrates: 11.4g; Protein: 56.1g

Ground Beef Tacos

Serves: 4
Preparation Time: 10 minutes
Cooking Time: 20 minutes
Ingredients:
1 pound ground beef
1 medium onion, finely chopped
2 garlic cloves, minced
1 cup beef broth
2 tbsp taco seasoning mix
1 tablespoon olive oil
8 small taco shells
Optional toppings: shredded lettuce, diced tomatoes, shredded cheese, sour cream, jalapeños, guacamole, salsa, and cilantro.

Directions:
1. Set your Instant Pot to SAUTÉ and add the olive oil.

2. Add the onion and sauté until it becomes translucent. Add the garlic and sauté for another minute.

3. Add the ground beef. Use a spatula to break up the meat and sauté until browned. Sprinkle the taco seasoning over the beef.

4. Pour in the beef broth, stirring well.

5. Close the lid, select the MANUAL or PRESSURE COOK setting, and cook at high pressure for 10 minutes.

6. When the cooking is complete, do a natural pressure release for 10 minutes. Quick release the remaining pressure.

7. Open the lid and give the beef mixture a good stir. With a slotted spoon, scoop the mixture into taco shells.

8. Add your desired toppings and serve immediately.

Nutritional Information (Per Serving)
Calories: 302; Fat: 18.5g; Net Carbohydrates: 15g; Protein: 16.5g

Balsamic Pot Roast

Serves: 6
Preparation Time: 5 minutes
Cooking Time: 45 minutes
Ingredients:
1 tablespoon sesame oil
3 pounds chuck roast
1 tablespoon salt
1 tablespoon garlic powder
1 tablespoon onion powder
¼ cup balsamic vinegar
2 cups water
1 medium onion, finely chopped
Some fresh parsley
Ground pepper to taste

Directions:
1. Lay the roast on a large plate. Season it with salt and pepper.
2. Heat the sesame oil in an Instant Pot on SAUTÉ and add the roast to it.
3. Fry the roast from both sides until thoroughly brown. Make sure not to burn it.
4. Pour some balsamic vinegar on top of the roast and cook it for about a minute.
5. Add onion and sauté for 2 minutes. Sprinkle some more salt, garlic powder, and onion powder and stir well. Press CANCEL.
6. Add the water, cover the lid, press the MANUAL or PRESSURE COOK setting, and cook at high pressure for 35 minutes.
7. When the cooking is complete, use a natural pressure release.
7. Garnish with some fresh parsley and serve.

Nutritional Information (Per Serving)
Calories: 528; Fat: 21.1g; Net Carbohydrates: 3.2g; Protein: 75.5g

Sweet and Sticky Short Ribs

Serves: 4
Preparation Time: 10 minutes
Cooking Time: 60 minutes
Ingredients:
1 tablespoon olive oil
2 teaspoons black pepper
4 short ribs, trimmed
1½ tablespoons garlic, chopped
2 tablespoons scallions, thinly sliced
½ cup water
1 tablespoon soy sauce
½ cup barbecue sauce
1½ tablespoons vinegar
1½ tablespoons brown sugar
1½ tablespoons red chili paste
2 tablespoons cold water
1 tablespoon cornstarch

Directions:
1. Program your Instant Pot to SAUTÉ. Add oil to the pot and heat the oil until it is warm.
2. Add short ribs and cook for 5 minutes until they turn brown. Afterward, place the short ribs on a plate.
3. Add garlic and scallions to the pot and cook for 1 minute, stirring constantly.
4. Add water, pepper, vinegar, barbecue sauce, sugar, soy sauce, and red chili paste, stirring the mixture to combine.
5. Close the lid and cook at high pressure for 45 minutes.
6. When the cooking is complete, do a quick pressure release. Carefully remove the ribs and place them aside.
7. Press SAUTÉ and simmer the sauce.
9. Whisk cold water and cornstarch in a small bowl. Add the mixture to the sauce and cook for about 1–2 minutes whisking constantly until it thickens.

10. Serve the cooked sauce over the short ribs and garnish with scallions.

Nutritional Information (Per Serving)
Calories: 1008; Fat: 86.6g; Net Carbohydrates: 20.3g; Protein: 33g

Instant Pot Pork Vindaloo

Serves: 6
Preparation Time: 15 minutes
Cooking Time: 45 minutes
Ingredients:
3 pounds trimmed pork butt roast
¾ teaspoon salt
Some ground pepper
2 tablespoons canola oil, divided
7 garlic cloves, minced
1 tablespoon paprika
1 teaspoon ground cumin
2 tablespoons red wine vinegar
1 tablespoon sugar
6 large tomatoes, chopped
Some cilantro leaves
3 medium onions, chopped
3 tablespoons all-purpose flour
1 cup water

Directions:
1. Set the Instant Pot to SAUTÉ and heat one tablespoon of oil in the Instant Pot.
2. Transfer pork to the pot and sauté for 7–8 minutes until it's brown on all sides. Set aside.
3. Heat the remaining oil in the pot. Throw in the minced garlic and onions and sauté until slightly brown.

4. Add the chopped tomatoes, paprika, ground cumin, and sugar and cook for about 2 minutes.

5. Add the flour and fry for a minute.

6. Now pour in the water, add vinegar, salt, and pepper, and stir the mixture well.

7. Add the browned pork, cover the lid of the pot, and cook at high pressure for 30 minutes.

8. Let the pressure release naturally and allow steam to escape.

9. Garnish with some cilantro and serve.

Nutritional Information (Per Serving)
Calories: 453; Fat: 13.3g; Net Carbohydrates: 15.2g; Protein: 62.4g

Pulled Pork Salad

Serves: 8
Preparation Time: 10 minutes
Cooking Time: 60 minutes

Pork Ingredients:
2 pounds pork butt
1 cup chicken broth
3 chipotle peppers
⅓ cup chili peppers, diced
¼ cup onions, minced
3 garlic cloves, diced
2 teaspoons olive oil
1 teaspoon cayenne pepper
½ teaspoon garlic powder
½ teaspoon cumin
Salt and pepper to taste

Salad Ingredients:
4 cups torn apart romaine lettuce
1 cup black beans
1 cup salsa fresca
½ cup plain yogurt
½ cup guacamole
Garnish with lime slices and cilantro

Directions:
1. In a bowl, mix the cayenne pepper, garlic powder, cumin, salt, and pepper together.
2. Rub the spice mix over the entire pork butt.
3. Set the Instant Pot on SAUTÉ. Add the olive oil and sauté the onion and garlic for 5 minutes.
4. Place the pork butt on top of the onion and garlic, and brown.
5. Transfer the pork butt to a platter.
6. Stir the broth, chili peppers, and chipotles into the Instant Pot.

7. Transfer the pork butt back into the Pot. Lock the lid, press MEAT, and cook for 50 minutes.

8. Transfer the pork butt to a platter and shred the meat. Stir the shredded meat back into the juices.

9. In a large bowl, mix the salad ingredients.

10. On serving plates, add the salad and top with shredded pork. Drizzle some of the juice over the salad.

Nutritional Information (Per Serving)
Calories: 309; Fat: 7.1g; Net Carbohydrates: 18.4g; Protein: 37.4g

Pork Wraps

Serves: 4
Preparation Time: 10 minutes
Cooking Time: 22 minutes
Ingredients:
2 pounds pork shoulder, chopped
1 tablespoon roasted and ground cumin
1 teaspoon ground pepper
1 teaspoon oregano
1 teaspoon ground cinnamon
3 garlic cloves, minced
1 dried chipotle pepper
1 cup tomatoes, diced
3 cups orange juice
1 teaspoon salt
Some lettuce, sliced cucumber pieces, sliced onion
4 tortillas

Directions:
1. Trim the fat from pork shoulder and add it to the Instant Pot. Add the rest of the ingredients except for the lettuce, cucumber, and onion. Mix well.

2. Close the lid and cook at high pressure for 20–22 minutes.

3. When the cooking is complete, use a natural pressure release. Transfer the mixture to a bowl.

4. Fill the tortillas with this mixture, layering with lettuce leaves, cucumbers, and onion slices.

5. Serve on a large plate.

Nutritional Information (Per Serving)
Calories: 824; Fat: 50.1g; Net Carbohydrates: 31.9g; Protein: 56.6g

Barbecue Pork Ribs

Serves: 6
Preparation Time: 10 minutes
Cooking Time: 45 minutes
Ingredients:
12 boneless country-style pork ribs (about 4 pounds)
1 cup ketchup
8 ounces pineapples, crushed with juices
2 tablespoons Worcestershire sauce
5 tablespoons brown sugar
2 teaspoons ginger, grated
¼ cup onion, minced
Dash of cayenne pepper
1 tablespoon cornstarch mixed with 2 tablespoons cold water

Ingredients for Spice Rub:
1 teaspoon garlic powder
1 teaspoon onion powder
Salt and pepper to taste
1 tablespoon Worcestershire sauce
2 tablespoons olive oil

Directions:

1. In a bowl, combine pineapples, sugar, ketchup, Worcestershire sauce, onions, ginger, and cayenne pepper. Set the bowl aside.
2. In another bowl, mix the spices for the rub.
3. Coat the ribs with the spice rub.
4. Set the Instant Pot to SAUTÉ and heat the olive oil.
5. Brown the ribs in batches and keep them on a plate.
6. Transfer all browned ribs back into the Instant Pot. Pour the pineapple sauce over the meat and stir well.
7. Shut the lid and cook at high pressure for 25 minutes.
8. After the beep, release pressure with the natural release.
9. Use tongs to transfer ribs to a platter. Cover and keep warm.
10. Use the SAUTÉ option to let the sauce come to a boil. Stir in cornstarch slurry and keep stirring until the sauce thickens.
11. Return the ribs to the Instant Pot and simmer in the sauce for 10 minutes.
12. Serve the ribs with rice or noodles and drizzle with the sauce.

Nutritional Information (Per Serving)
Calories: 971; Fat: 58.4g; Net Carbohydrates: 25.7g; Protein: 81.2g

Super Sausage and Peppers

Serves: 4
Preparation Time: 5 minutes
Cooking Time: 50 minutes
Ingredients:
4 sweet Italian sausages
4 spicy Italian sausages
4 large bell peppers (any color)
1 15-ounce can diced tomatoes
1 15-ounce jar tomato sauce
1 cup water
1 red onion
4 cloves garlic, minced
2 tablespoons dried Italian seasoning

Directions:

1. Pour the tomatoes (with juices) and the tomato sauce into the Instant Pot.

2. Add the water, garlic, and Italian seasoning.

3. Chop the peppers and the onion into strips or chunks.

4. Add the sausages to the Instant Pot and top them with the peppers and onions.

5. Lock the lid into place and cook at high pressure for 20 minutes.

6. When the cooking is complete, use a natural pressure release.

Nutritional Information (Per Serving)
Calories: 370; Fat: 17g; Net Carbohydrates: 21.6g; Protein: 31.2g

Braised Lamb Shanks

Serves: 4
Preparation Time: 10 minutes
Cooking Time: 35 minutes
Ingredients:
2 pounds lamb shanks
4 tablespoons white flour
2 tablespoons olive oil
2 garlic cloves, diced
1 large onion, chopped
3 carrots, diced
2 tablespoons tomato paste
1 tomato, diced
1 teaspoon oregano
1 cup red wine
½ cup beef stock
Salt and pepper to taste

Directions:
1. In a shallow bowl, mix the flour, salt, and pepper.
2. Dredge the lamb shanks through the flour.
3. Set the Instant Pot to SAUTÉ and add the olive oil.
4. Sauté the lamb until browned and transfer to a plate.
5. In the remaining hot oil, sauté the garlic and onion for 5 minutes.
6. Mix in the tomato paste, diced tomato, red wine, and beef stock. Stir well and bring the mixture to a boil.
7. Return the lamb shanks to the Instant Pot. Shut the lid and cook at low pressure for 25 minutes.
8. When the cooking is complete, use a natural pressure release.
9. Transfer the lamb shanks to a platter and top with cooking liquid.

Nutritional Information (Per Serving)
Calories: 609; Fat: 24g; Net Carbohydrates: 15.6g; Protein: 66.5g

Garlicky Lamb

Serves: 4
Preparation Time: 5 minutes
Cooking Time: 25 minutes
Ingredients:
1 tablespoon butter
1 tablespoon olive oil
6 garlic cloves, peeled
2 pounds lamb shanks
½ teaspoon thyme
1 tablespoon balsamic vinegar
1 cup chicken broth
1 tablespoon tomato paste

Directions:
1. Set your Instant Pot to SAUTÉ and heat the olive oil.
2. Add garlic cloves and cook until they become browned.
3. Stir in the tomato paste, vinegar, chicken broth, and thyme.
4. Add the lamb shank and close the lid.
5. Set the Instant Pot to the MANUAL or PRESSURE COOK setting and cook at high pressure for 20 minutes.
6. Release the pressure naturally.
7. Transfer the lamb shanks to a plate.
8. Whisk the butter and balsamic into the pot.
9. Drizzle the sauce over the lamb.
10. Serve and enjoy!

Nutritional Information (Per Serving)
Calories: 498; Fat: 23.4g; Net Carbohydrates: 3g; Protein: 65.5g

Rosemary Lamb Chops

Serves: 4
Preparation Time: 15 minutes
Cooking Time: 15 minutes
Ingredients:
4 lamb chops
1½ tbsp fresh rosemary, finely chopped
2 cloves garlic, minced
1 cup beef broth
2 tbsp olive oil
Salt and pepper to taste
Zest of 1 lemon
1 tbsp lemon juice
Fresh rosemary sprigs for garnish

Directions:
1. Season both sides of the lamb chops with salt, pepper, rosemary, garlic, and lemon zest.
2. Set your Instant Pot to SAUTÉ and add the olive oil.
3. Place the lamb chops in the pot (you may have to do this in batches). Sear each side for 2–3 minutes or until browned. Remove the lamb chops and set aside.
4. Pour in the beef broth and lemon juice and return the lamb chops to the pot.
5. Close the lid, select the MANUAL or PRESSURE COOK setting, and cook at high pressure for 7 minutes.
6. When the cooking is complete, do a natural pressure release for 10 minutes. Quick release the remaining pressure.
7. Garnish with fresh rosemary sprigs and serve hot.

Nutritional Information (Per Serving)
Calories: 367; Fat: 31g; Net Carbohydrates: 0g; Protein: 23g

Flank Steak

Serves: 4
Preparation Time: 15 minutes
Cooking Time: 23 minutes
Ingredients:
1 pound flank steaks, trimmed and cut into ¼-inch thick strips
Salt and pepper to taste
½ tablespoon olive oil
2 garlic cloves, minced
¼ cup water
¼ cup coconut aminos
2 tablespoons fresh lemon juice
1 tablespoon raw honey
1 tablespoon arrowroot starch
1½ tablespoons cold water
2 tablespoons fresh parsley, chopped

Directions:
1. Season the steak with salt and pepper evenly.
2. Place the oil in the Instant Pot and select SAUTÉ. Add the steak, salt, and pepper, and cook for about 5 minutes.
3. Transfer the beef to a bowl.
4. In the pot, add garlic and sauté for about 1 minute.
5. Press CANCEL and stir in beef, ¼ cup of water, coconut aminos, lemon juice, and honey.
6. Close the lid, select the MANUAL or PRESSURE COOK setting, and cook at high pressure for 12 minutes.
7. When the cooking is complete, do a quick pressure release.
8. Meanwhile, in a small bowl, dissolve the arrowroot starch in cold water.
9. Open the lid and select SAUTÉ.
10. Add the arrowroot mixture to the Instant Pot, stirring continuously. Cook for 4–5 minutes or until desired thickness.
11. Stir in parsley and serve hot.

Nutritional Information (Per Serving)

Calories: 278; Fat: 11.3g; Net Carbohydrates: 9.7g; Protein: 31.8g

Feta Meatloaf

Serves: 6
Preparation Time: 10 minutes
Cooking Time: 23 minutes
Ingredients:
1 small yellow onion, chopped roughly
6–8 garlic cloves, chopped
2 teaspoons fresh rosemary
2 teaspoons fresh marjoram
Salt and pepper to taste
2 pounds ground beef
¼ cup feta cheese, crumbled

Directions:
1. In a food processor, add onion and pulse until finely chopped.
2. Place chopped onion in a paper towel and squeeze out all the liquid.
3. Return the onion to the food processor with garlic, herbs, salt, and pepper and pulse until garlic is minced.
4. Add ground beef and pulse until well combined.
5. Place mixture into a loaf pan and press firmly.
6. Cover the loaf pan with a piece of foil tightly and with a fork, poke a few vent holes in the foil.
7. In the bottom of the Instant Pot, arrange a steamer trivet and pour 1 cup of water.
8. Arrange the meatloaf on top of the trivet.
9. Close the lid, select the MANUAL or PRESSURE COOK setting, and cook at high pressure for 20 minutes.
10. When the cooking is complete, use a natural pressure release.
11. Preheat the broiler of the oven.

12. Remove the loaf pan and place it onto a wire rack to cool for about 15 minutes.

13. Carefully, remove the meatloaf from the pan and transfer it onto a broiler pan. Broil for 2–3 minutes.

14. Remove from oven and immediately, top with feta cheese.

15. Cut into desired-sized slices and serve.

Nutritional Information (Per Serving)
Calories: 310; Fat: 10.9g; Net Carbohydrates: 2.5g; Protein: 47.2g

CHAPTER FIVE

Fish and Seafood

Cod with Parsley and Peas

Serves: 4
Preparation Time: 10 minutes
Cooking Time: 10 minutes
Ingredients:
1 pound cod, cut into 4 filets
1 bag (10 ounces) frozen peas
1 cup fresh parsley
1 cup white wine
2 garlic cloves, smashed
1 teaspoon paprika
1 teaspoon oregano
1 sprig fresh rosemary
Salt and pepper to taste

Directions:

1. In a small bowl, stir the wine, herbs, salt, and spices together until blended.

2. Pour the liquid into the Instant Pot and add the frozen peas.

3. Place the fish into a steamer basket and close the lid. Cook at high pressure for 5 minutes.

4. When the cooking is complete, do a quick pressure release.

5. The peas will be mushy and soft, so plate those first. Serve the fish on top.

Nutritional Information (Per Serving)
Calories: 234; Fat: 1.4g; Net Carbohydrates: 8.9g; Protein: 30.3g

Vietnamese Salmon

Serves: 4
Preparation Time: 15 minutes
Cooking Time: 15 minutes
Ingredients:
4 salmon fillets
3 cloves garlic, minced
1 tablespoon fresh ginger, grated
2 tablespoons fish sauce
2 tablespoons soy sauce
3 tablespoons brown sugar
Black pepper to taste
1 tablespoon lime juice
¼ cup green onions, sliced (for garnish)
1 tablespoon vegetable oil
½ cup water

Directions:
1. In a bowl, combine the garlic, ginger, fish sauce, soy sauce, brown sugar, black pepper, and lime juice. Whisk until the sugar is dissolved.
2. Place the salmon fillets in the marinade for at least 30 minutes in the refrigerator.
3. Set your Instant Pot to SAUTÉ and add the vegetable oil.
4. Place the salmon fillets skin-side down (reserve the marinade). Sear the salmon for about 2 minutes on each side or until they get a light golden crust.
5. Pour the reserved marinade over the salmon. Add ½ cup of water around the salmon.
6. Close the lid, choose the MANUAL or PRESSURE COOK setting, and cook at low pressure for 5 minutes.
7. When the cooking is complete, do a quick pressure release.
8. Garnish with green onions and serve with steamed jasmine rice or rice noodles.

Nutritional Information (Per Serving)

Calories: 300; Fat: 16g; Net Carbohydrates: 7g; Protein: 28g

Seafood Gumbo

Serves: 10
Preparation Time: 15 minutes
Cooking Time: 19 minutes
Ingredients:
1 cup flour
¾ cup canola oil
1 onion, sliced
2 celery stalks, diced
1 cup green pepper, diced
3 garlic cloves, minced
3 tablespoons peanut oil
5 medium tomatoes, peeled and diced
2 bay leaves
1 teaspoon cayenne pepper
½ teaspoon garlic powder
1 teaspoon paprika
1 teaspoon thyme
1 pound Italian sausage, sliced
8 cups chicken stock
16 peeled raw shrimps without tails
20 cooked crawfish
3 cups lump crab meat
16 shucked oysters
Salt and pepper to taste

Directions:
1. Heat a skillet over medium heat, stir the flour and vegetable oil together for 3–4 minutes. (This is a roux.) Set aside.
2. Add the peanut oil to the Instant Pot and activate the SAUTÉ function. Cook the peppers, onions, and garlic for 5 minutes.
3. Stir in the tomatoes, sausage, stock, and all of the spices.

4. Spoon in the roux while stirring.

5. Add all the seafood to the Instant Pot. Shut the lid and cook at high pressure for 8–10 minutes.

6. Release pressure naturally.

7. Serve Gumbo with rice.

Nutritional Information (Per Serving)
Calories: 495; Fat: 35.9g; Net Carbohydrates: 13.6g; Protein: 27.5g

Coconut Fish Curry

Serves: 5
Preparation Time: 15 minutes
Cooking Time: 15 minutes
Ingredients:
1½ pounds fish steak, cut into small pieces
1 tablespoon coconut oil
1 teaspoon minced ginger
2 garlic cloves, minced
2 medium onions, sliced
Some curry leaves
¼ teaspoon turmeric
2 teaspoons ground cumin
1 teaspoon coriander powder
1 teaspoon chili powder
2 small green chilies, slit open
1 cup cherry tomatoes
2 cups coconut milk
¾ teaspoon salt
1 tablespoon lemon juice

Directions:
1. Set the Instant Pot to SAUTÉ and heat the coconut oil.

2. Add the curry leaves, ginger, garlic, and onion and fry for 2–3 minutes.

3. Add the turmeric powder, ground cumin, coriander powder, and chili powder and mix well.

4. Slide in the chilies and cherry tomatoes and sauté for another 2 minutes.

5. Pour in the coconut milk, add the salt and lemon juice, and bring to a boil.

6. Add the fish steaks and stir the mixture.

7. Cover the lid and cook for 5–7 minutes at high pressure.

8. When the cooking is complete, do a quick pressure release.

9. Serve hot.

Nutritional Information (Per Serving)
Calories: 581; Fat: 41.6g; Net Carbohydrates: 31.2g; Protein: 17.5g

Tuna Steaks with Capers

Serves: 4
Preparation Time: 10 minutes
Cooking Time: 10 minutes
Ingredients:
4 tuna steaks
1 tablespoon olive oil
¼ cup white wine
¼ cup chicken broth
3 tablespoons capers, drained
2 cloves garlic, minced
1 tablespoon fresh lemon juice
Zest of 1 lemon
2 tablespoons fresh parsley, finely chopped
Salt and pepper to taste

Directions:
1. Season the tuna steaks on both sides with salt and pepper.
2. Set your Instant Pot to SAUTÉ and add the olive oil.
3. Add the tuna steaks and sear for 1 minute on each side.
4. Remove the tuna steaks and set aside. Add garlic to the pot and sauté for about 30 seconds, until fragrant.
5. Add the white wine, chicken broth, capers, lemon juice, and lemon zest. Mix well.
6. Insert a trivet in the Instant Pot. Place the tuna steaks on the trivet.
7. Close the lid, choose the MANUAL or PRESSURE COOK setting, and cook at low pressure for 5 minutes.
8. When the cooking is complete, do a quick pressure release.
9. Garnish with fresh parsley and serve.

Nutritional Information (Per Serving)
Calories: 263; Fat: 9g; Net Carbohydrates: 0.2g; Protein: 40g

Shrimp Fried Rice

Serves: 6
Preparation Time: 10 minutes
Cooking Time: 35 minutes
Ingredients:
3 tablespoons sesame oil
2 large eggs
2 medium red onions, chopped
4 garlic cloves, minced
2 cups frozen shrimp, washed and tailed
1 cup peas
1 cup carrots
2 tablespoons soy sauce
2 cups brown rice
4 cups water
½ teaspoon cayenne pepper
1 tablespoon apple cider vinegar
½ teaspoon salt
1 teaspoon ginger, minced

Directions:
1. Set the Instant Pot on SAUTÉ and let it heat up for 2 minutes.
2. Add the sesame oil. Throw in the minced garlic and chopped onion and sauté until the onion turns slightly brown.
3. Slide in the chopped carrots and peas and fry for 4–5 minutes.
4. Add the shrimp, minced ginger, soy sauce, water, salt, pepper, and vinegar, and let simmer for 3–4 minutes.
5. Rinse the brown rice with water and add it to the pot.
6. Crack two eggs into the mixture and stir well. Cover the lid and press RICE.
7. When the cooking is complete, do a natural pressure release for 10 minutes. Quick release the remaining pressure.
8. Transfer the rice to a large plate and serve.

Nutritional Information (Per Serving)

Calories: 479; Fat: 12.3g; Net Carbohydrates: 54.6g; Protein: 31.5g

Spicy Shrimp

Serves: 4
Preparation Time: 10 minutes
Cooking Time: 5 minutes
Ingredients:
1 pound frozen shrimp, peeled and deveined
1 lemon, juiced
1 teaspoon black pepper
1 teaspoon white pepper
1 teaspoon cayenne pepper
1 can diced tomatoes (14–15 ounces)
1 jalapeno pepper, minced
2 cloves garlic, minced
1 sweet onion, minced

Directions:
1. Pour the tomatoes and juices into the Instant Pot.
2. Add the lemon juice, garlic, and onion and stir.
3. Allow the frozen shrimp to rest at room temperature for 15 minutes. Then, add them to the Instant Pot.
4. Add the jalapeno and the black, white, and cayenne peppers.
5. Mix everything. Cook at low pressure for 5 minutes.
6. When the cooking is complete, do a quick pressure release.

Nutritional Information (Per Serving)
Calories: 174; Fat: 2.3g; Net Carbohydrates: 8.2g; Protein: 27.4g

Paprika Shrimp Stew

Serves: 4
Preparation Time: 15 minutes
Cooking Time: 20 minutes
Ingredients:
1 pound large shrimp, peeled and deveined
1 medium onion, diced
3 cloves garlic, minced
1 red bell pepper, diced
1 green bell pepper, diced
2 tablespoons tomato paste
1 can (14½ ounces) diced tomatoes, undrained
1 tablespoon smoked paprika
¼ teaspoon cayenne pepper
Salt and pepper to taste
2 cups chicken broth
1 lemon, zested and juiced
2 tablespoons fresh parsley, chopped (for garnish)

Directions:
1. In the Instant Pot, combine all of the ingredients except for the fresh parsley.
2. Cover the lid, choose the MANUAL or PRESSURE COOK setting, and cook at low pressure for 5 minutes.
3. When the cooking is complete, do a quick pressure release.
4. Garnish with parsley and serve hot.

Nutritional Information (Per Serving)
Calories: 171; Fat: 2g; Net Carbohydrates: 8g; Protein: 23g

Mediterranean Calamari

Serves: 6
Preparation Time: 10 minutes
Cooking Time: 4 minutes
Ingredients:
2 pounds calamari, chopped
2 tablespoons olive oil
1 red onion, sliced
3 cloves of garlic, chopped
1 cup red wine
3 stalks of celery, chopped
1 can (28 ounces) crushed tomatoes
3 sprigs fresh rosemary
½ cup Italian parsley, chopped
Salt and pepper to taste

Directions:
1. Toss the calamari pieces in olive oil and salt and pepper.
2. To the Instant Pot, add the wine, tomatoes with their juices, celery, rosemary, garlic, and red onion.
3. Place the calamari in a steamer basket and lower it to the liquid. Cook at high pressure for 4 minutes.
4. When the cooking is complete, use a natural pressure release.
5. Remove the fish and sprinkle with fresh parsley.

Nutritional Information (Per Serving)
Calories: 155; Fat: 5.5g; Net Carbohydrates: 4.9g; Protein: 12.4g

Orange Salmon

Serves: 4
Preparation Time: 10 minutes
Cooking Time: 5 minutes
Ingredients:
1½ pounds salmon fillets
1 cup water
Salt and pepper to taste
4 teaspoons olive oil
1 medium onion, chopped
5 tablespoons parsley, chopped
2 teaspoons orange rind
Orange slices

Directions:
1. Insert a trivet in the Instant Pot and add the water.
2. Season the salmon fillets with salt, pepper, and olive oil, and arrange them on the trivet.
3. Place onion, parsley, and orange rinds on top of the salmon.
4. Close the lid, choose the MANUAL or PRESSURE COOK setting, and cook at low pressure for 5 minutes.
5. When the cooking is complete, do a quick pressure release.
6. Garnish with orange slices and serve.

Nutritional Information (Per Serving)
Calories: 279; Fat: 15.2g; Net Carbohydrates: 2.2g; Protein: 33.4g

Steamed Salmon

Serves: 4
Preparation Time: 5 minutes
Cooking Time: 15 minutes
Ingredients:
4 salmon filets
2 cups water
4 Roma tomatoes
2 lemons
½ cup chopped shallots
4 sprigs fresh rosemary
1 tablespoon olive oil
Salt and pepper to taste

Directions:
1. Slice the tomatoes and the lemons.
2. Make two foil pouches with two pieces of salmon each. Lay the salmon down on the foil and cover with salt and pepper, olive oil, a layer of tomatoes, a layer of lemons, a sprinkle of shallots, and a sprig of rosemary. Fold up the foil so it creates a secure little package.
3. Pour the water into the Instant Pot, place the salmon into a steamer basket, and lower the basket to the pot.
4. Cook at low pressure for 10 minutes.
5. When the cooking is complete, do a quick pressure release.
6. Carefully unfold the packets and serve.

Nutritional Information (Per Serving)
Calories: 495; Fat: 22.9g; Net Carbohydrates: 11.6g; Protein: 55.9g

Fish Chowder

Serves: 6
Preparation Time: 10 minutes
Cooking Time: 25 minutes
Ingredients:
2 pounds cod
2 tablespoons butter
1 onion, diced
1 cup mushrooms, sliced
2 pounds potatoes, peeled and cubed
3 cups chicken broth
1 cup water
1½ teaspoons Old Bay Seasoning
1 cup clam juice
½ cup flour
1½ cups evaporated milk

Directions:
1. Insert a trivet in the Instant Pot and fill it with a cup of water.
2. Cut the fish into bite-sized pieces and transfer to the trivet.
3. Shut the lid and the valve. Cook at high pressure for 9 minutes.
4. Release pressure naturally. Transfer the fish to a platter.
5. Toss the liquid left in the pot and take out the trivet.
6. Set the Instant Pot on SAUTÉ and cook the mushrooms and onions in the butter for 2 minutes.
7. Stir in the broth, water, and potatoes, then shut the lid and the valve. Cook at high pressure for 8 minutes.
8. When the Instant Pot beeps, press CANCEL and release the pressure naturally.
9. Add the fish, salt, pepper, and Old Bay Seasoning. Set the Instant Pot to SAUTÉ.
10. Mix the flour and the clam juice together and add to the stew. Bring to a boil.
11. Switch the Instant Pot off, pour in the evaporated milk and stir.

Nutritional Information (Per Serving)
Calories: 426; Fat: 8.6g; Net Carbohydrates: 37.2g; Protein: 43.6g

Fish Curry

Serves: 4
Preparation Time: 15 minutes
Cooking Time: 11 minutes
Ingredients:
2 tablespoons olive oil
2 medium onions, chopped
2 teaspoons fresh ginger, grated finely
4 garlic cloves, minced
2 tablespoons curry powder
2 teaspoons ground cumin
2 teaspoons ground coriander
1 teaspoon red chili powder
½ teaspoon ground turmeric
2 cups unsweetened coconut milk
1½ pounds fish fillets, cut into bite-sized pieces
1 cup tomatoes, chopped
2 Serrano peppers, seeded and chopped
1 tablespoon fresh lemon juice

Directions:
1. Place the oil in the Instant Pot and select SAUTÉ. Add the onion, ginger, and garlic and cook for 4–5 minutes.
2. Add the spices and cook for 1 minute.
3. Add the coconut milk and stir to combine well.
4. Press CANCEL and stir in the fish, tomatoes, and Serrano pepper.
5. Secure the lid and cook at low pressure for 5 minutes.
6. When cooking is complete, use a natural pressure release.
7. Remove the lid and stir in the lemon juice.

8. Serve hot.

Nutritional Information (Per Serving)
Calories: 787; Fat: 57.6g; Net Carbohydrates: 40.2g; Protein: 29.7g

Ginger-Lemon Haddock

Serves: 4
Preparation Time: 5 minutes
Cooking Time: 50 minutes
Ingredients:
4 filets of haddock
2 lemons
1-inch fresh ginger, chopped
4 green onions
1 cup white wine
Salt and pepper to taste
2 tablespoons olive oil

Directions:
1. Massage the olive oil into the fish filets and sprinkle them with salt and pepper.
2. Juice your lemons and zest one of them.
3. Add that to the Instant Pot with the wine, onions, and ginger.
4. Place the fish in a steamer basket and lower it to the liquid.
5. Close the lid and cook at high pressure for 8 minutes.
6. When the cooking is complete, do a quick pressure release.
7. Remove the fish and serve on rice or with a big salad.

Nutritional Information (Per Serving)
Calories: 274; Fat: 8.7g; Net Carbohydrates: 4.4g; Protein: 32.2g

Steamed Mussels

Serves: 3
Preparation Time: 5 minutes
Cooking Time: 3 minutes
Ingredients:
3 pounds fresh mussels, cleaned and rinsed
1 can diced tomatoes (14 ounces)
1 cup white wine
1 tablespoon pepper
1 tablespoon dried parsley

Directions:
1. Pour the tomatoes into the Instant Pot with the juices and add the wine. Stir together and add the pepper and parsley.
2. Place the mussels in a steamer basket and lower it to the liquid.
3. Close the lid and cook at high pressure for 3 minutes.
4. When the cooking is complete, do a quick pressure release.
5. Cover the mussels with the tomato and wine sauce. Serve with garlic bread.

Nutritional Information (Per Serving)
Calories: 472; Fat: 10.4g; Net Carbohydrates: 21.4g; Protein: 54.8g

Flounder Piccata

Serves: 4
Preparation Time: 15 minutes
Cooking Time: 10 minutes
Ingredients:
4 flounder fillets
Salt and pepper to taste
¼ cup all-purpose flour, for dredging
3 tablespoons olive oil
3 cloves garlic, minced
¼ cup fresh lemon juice
½ cup chicken broth
¼ cup capers, rinsed and drained
2 tablespoons unsalted butter
2 tablespoons fresh parsley, chopped

Directions:
1. Season both sides of the flounder fillets with salt and pepper. Dredge each fillet lightly in the flour, shaking off the excess.
2. Set your Instant Pot to SAUTÉ and add 2 tablespoons of the olive oil.
3. Add the flounder fillets (in batches if necessary) and sear for 1–2 minutes per side or until lightly golden. Remove the fillets and set aside.
4. Add the remaining tablespoon of olive oil, followed by the minced garlic. Sauté for about 30 seconds or until fragrant.
5. Pour in the lemon juice and chicken broth. Add the capers.
6. Return the flounder fillets to the Instant Pot, placing them on top of the liquid.
7. Close the lid, choose the MANUAL or PRESSURE COOK setting, and cook at low pressure for 5 minutes.
8. When the cooking is complete, do a quick pressure release.
9. Garnish with chopped parsley and serve immediately.

Nutritional Information (Per Serving)
Calories: 269; Fat: 17g; Net Carbohydrates: 7g; Protein: 21g

Fish and Tomatoes

Serves: 6
Preparation Time: 15 minutes
Cooking Time: 5 minutes
Total Time: 20 minutes
Ingredients:
3 pounds cod
1 large onion, sliced
1½ cans (15 ounces each) diced tomatoes
⅓ cup low sodium broth
Salt, pepper, and red pepper flakes to taste
1 large bell pepper, sliced
5 cloves garlic, minced
1½ tablespoons rosemary
Seasoning of your choice, as required

Directions:
1. Set aside the fish and seasoning and add the rest of the ingredients into the Instant Pot. Mix well.
2. Sprinkle seasoning all over the fish as well as on the mixture. Place fish on the mixture.
3. Close the lid, select the MANUAL or PRESSURE COOK setting, and cook at high pressure for 5 minutes.
4. When the cooking is complete, do a quick pressure release.

Nutritional Information (Per Serving)
Calories: 277; Fat: 2.4g; Net Carbohydrates: 6.5g; Protein: 53.1g

Mahi-Mahi in Tomato Sauce

Serves: 6
Preparation Time: 15 minutes
Cooking Time: 14 minutes
Total Time: 29 minutes
Ingredients:
3 tablespoons butter
1 (28-ounce) can diced tomatoes, no sugar added
1 yellow onion, sliced
2 tablespoons fresh lemon juice
1 teaspoon dried oregano
Salt and pepper to taste
6 (4-ounce) mahi-mahi fillets

Directions:
1. Place the butter in the Instant Pot and select SAUTÉ. Add all ingredients except fish fillets and cook for 8–10 minutes.
2. Press CANCEL and place fish fillets over the sauce. With a spoon, place some sauce over the fillets.
3. Close the lid, select the MANUAL or PRESSURE COOK setting, and cook at high pressure for 4 minutes.
4. When the cooking is complete, do a quick pressure release.
5. Serve hot with the topping of sauce.

Nutritional Information (Per Serving)
Calories: 180; Fat: 6.9g; Net Carbohydrates: 5g; Protein: 22.5g

CHAPTER SIX

Vegetables and Beans

Spiced Okra

Serves: 4
Preparation Time: 15 minutes
Cooking Time: 10 minutes
Ingredients:
2 tablespoons olive oil
6 garlic cloves, chopped
1 teaspoon cumin seeds
2 medium onions, sliced
2 medium tomatoes, chopped
2 pounds okra, cut into 1-inch pieces
½ cup vegetable broth
1 teaspoon ground coriander
½ teaspoon red chili powder
½ teaspoon ground turmeric
Salt and pepper to taste

Directions:
1. Place the olive oil in the Instant Pot and select SAUTÉ. Add the garlic and cumin seeds and cook for 1 minute.
2. Add the onion and cook for 4 minutes.
3. Add the remaining ingredients and cook for 1 more minute.
4. Press CANCEL and stir well.
5. Secure the lid and cook at high pressure for 2 minutes.
6. When the cooking is complete, do a quick pressure release.
7. Serve hot.

Nutritional Information (Per Serving)
Calories: 195; Fat: 7.8g; Net Carbohydrates: 17g; Protein: 6g

Vegetable Medley

Serves: 6
Preparation Time: 15 minutes
Cooking Time: 10 minutes
Ingredients:
2 cups broccoli florets
2 cups cauliflower florets
1 cup carrots, sliced
1 cup green beans, trimmed and cut into 2-inch lengths
1 red bell pepper, seeded and cut into strips
1 cup zucchini, sliced
2 tablespoons olive oil
3 cloves garlic, minced
1 teaspoon dried Italian seasoning
½ cup vegetable broth
Salt and pepper to taste
Fresh parsley, chopped for garnish

Directions:
1. Set your Instant Pot to SAUTÉ and add the olive oil.
2. Add the garlic and sauté for about 30 seconds or until fragrant.
3. Add the broccoli, cauliflower, carrots, and green beans. Sauté for 2–3 minutes.
4. Sprinkle the dried Italian seasoning over the vegetables. Season with salt and pepper.
5. Pour in the vegetable broth and add the red bell pepper and zucchini on top.
6. Secure the lid and cook at high pressure for 2 minutes.
7. When the cooking is complete, carefully do a quick pressure release.
8. Garnish with fresh parsley and serve warm.

Nutritional Information (Per Serving)
Calories: 89; Fat: 4.8g; Net Carbohydrates: 8.6g; Protein: 2.6g

Corn Chowder

Serves: 6
Preparation Time: 10 minutes
Cooking Time: 10 minutes
Ingredients:
3 cups frozen corn
2 cups chicken broth
3 medium potatoes, chopped
1 onion, chopped
Salt and pepper to taste
2 tablespoons butter
2 cups milk

Directions:
1. Add the first 5 ingredients to the Instant Pot. Stir everything together.
2. Close the lid, choose MANUAL, and cook at high pressure for 7 minutes.
3. When the cooking is complete, press CANCEL, and do a quick pressure release.
4. Open the lid, and blend the mixture with a hand blender, until smooth.
5. Set the pot to SAUTÉ. Add the butter and milk, and stir to combine. Let it simmer for 2 minutes.
6. Serve warm.

Nutritional Information (Per Serving)
Calories: 234; Fat: 7g; Net Carbohydrates: 32.1g; Protein: 8.8g

Creamed Kale

Serves: 4
Preparation Time: 10 minutes
Cooking Time: 12 minutes
Ingredients:
1 tablespoon olive oil
1 medium onion, finely chopped
2 cloves garlic, minced
1 cup heavy cream
4 cups kale, stems removed and chopped
½ cup vegetable broth
½ cup grated Parmesan cheese
¼ teaspoon ground nutmeg
Salt and pepper to taste

Directions:
1. Set your Instant Pot to SAUTÉ and add the olive oil.
2. Add the onion and sauté until it becomes translucent. Add the garlic and sauté for another minute.
3. Add the kale to the pot. You may need to add them in batches, letting each batch wilt down a bit before adding more.
4. Pour in the vegetable broth.
5. Close the lid, select the MANUAL or PRESSURE COOK setting, and cook at high pressure for 4 minutes.
6. When the cooking is complete, do a quick pressure release.
7. Open the lid, and set the Instant Pot to SAUTÉ. Add the heavy cream, grated Parmesan cheese, ground nutmeg, salt, and pepper. Stir well. Allow the mixture to simmer for 3–4 minutes.
8. Serve immediately.

Nutritional Information (Per Serving)
Calories: 342; Fat: 30.1g; Net Carbohydrates: 13g; Protein: 8.9g

Beet Salad

Serves: 4
Preparation Time: 15 minutes
Cooking Time: 25 minutes
Ingredients:
For Salad:
8 medium beets, trimmed
4 cups fresh baby spinach
2 tablespoons balsamic vinegar
2 tablespoons feta cheese, crumbled

For Dressing:
4 tablespoons capers
1 garlic clove, minced
2 tablespoons fresh parsley, minced
2 tablespoons extra-virgin olive oil
Salt and pepper to taste

Directions:
1. Arrange the trivet in the Instant Pot. Add 1 cup of water to the Instant Pot.
2. Place the beets on top of the trivet in a single layer.
3. Secure the lid and cook at high pressure for 20 minutes.
4. When the cooking is complete, do a quick pressure release.
5. Remove the inner pot and rinse the beet under running cold water.
6. Cut the beets into desired-size slices and transfer into a salad bowl.
7. Add spinach and drizzle with vinegar.
8. In a bowl, add all dressing ingredients and beat until well combined.
9. Pour dressing over beets mixture and gently toss to coat well.
10. Serve with the topping of cheese.

Nutritional Information (Per Serving)
Calories: 174; Fat: 8.6g; Net Carbohydrates: 17.3g; Protein: 5.3g

Zucchini with Tomatoes

Serves: 4
Preparation Time: 10 minutes
Cooking Time: 10 minutes
Ingredients:
3 medium zucchinis, sliced
2 large tomatoes, diced
1 medium onion, finely chopped
3 garlic cloves, minced
2 tablespoons olive oil
½ teaspoon dried basil
½ teaspoon dried oregano
Salt and pepper to taste
¼ cup vegetable broth

Directions:
1. Set your Instant Pot to SAUTÉ and add the olive oil.
2. Add the onion and sauté until it becomes translucent. Add the garlic and sauté for another minute.
3. Add the zucchinis, tomatoes, dried herbs, salt, and pepper. Stir to mix well.
4. Pour the vegetable broth into the Instant Pot.
5. Close the lid, choose the MANUAL or PRESSURE COOK setting, and cook at low pressure for 5 minutes.
6. When the cooking is complete, do a natural pressure release for 5 minutes. Quick release the remaining pressure.
7. Serve warm.

Nutritional Information (Per Serving)
Calories: 103; Fat: 7.2g; Net Carbohydrates: 8.9g; Protein: 2g

Brussels Sprout Salad

Serves: 4
Preparation Time: 15 minutes
Cooking Time: 5 minutes
Ingredients:
1 pound Brussels sprouts, trimmed and halved
1 tablespoon unsalted butter, melted
1 cup pomegranate seeds
½ cup almonds, chopped

Directions:
1. Arrange the steamer basket at the bottom of the Instant Pot. Add 1 cup of water to the Instant Pot.
2. Arrange the Brussels sprout in the steamer basket.
3. Secure the lid and cook at high pressure for 4 minutes.
4. When the cooking is complete, carefully do a quick pressure release.
5. Remove the lid, transfer the Brussels sprouts onto serving plates, and drizzle with the melted butter.
6. Top with pomegranate seeds and almonds and serve.

Nutritional Information (Per Serving)
Calories: 174; Fat: 9.2g; Net Carbohydrates: 14.1g; Protein: 6.7g

Lentil Tacos

Serves: 4
Preparation Time: 5 minutes
Cooking Time: 15 minutes
Ingredients:
2 cups lentils
4 cups water
3 tablespoons tomato paste
¾ teaspoon salt
1 teaspoon chili powder
1 teaspoon onion powder
1 teaspoon garlic powder
4 tacos
½ teaspoon ground cumin
Some fresh lettuce leaves

Directions:

1. Add all the ingredients to the Instant Pot except the lettuce and tacos. Mix them well.

2. Close the lid and cook at high pressure for 15 minutes.

3. When the cooking is complete, do a natural pressure release for 10 minutes. Quick release the remaining pressure.

4. Carefully take out the mixture and place on a large plate.

5. Fill each of the tacos with the lentil mixture. Layer it with lettuce leaves and serve.

Nutritional Information (Per Serving)
Calories: 482; Fat: 21.2g; Net Carbohydrates: 43.6g; Protein: 27.1g

Garlicky Bell Peppers

Serves: 4
Preparation Time: 20 minutes
Cooking Time: 5 minutes
Ingredients:
2 tablespoons olive oil
8 garlic cloves, minced
2 jalapeño peppers, seeded and chopped
2 green bell peppers, seeded and cut into long strips
2 red bell peppers, seeded and cut into long strips
2 yellow bell peppers, seeded and cut into long strips
2 orange bell peppers, seeded and cut into long strips
Salt and pepper to taste
½ cup water
2 tablespoons fresh lemon juice

Directions:
1. Place the oil in the Instant Pot and select SAUTÉ. Add the garlic and jalapeño and cook for 1 minute.
2. Press CANCEL and stir in the remaining ingredients, except lemon juice.
3. Secure the lid and cook at high pressure for 2 minutes.
4. When the cooking is complete, use a quick pressure release.
5. Remove the lid and select SAUTÉ.
6. Stir in lemon juice and cook for 1–2 minutes.
7. Press CANCEL and serve.

Nutritional Information (Per Serving)
Calories: 149; Fat: 7.7g; Net Carbohydrates: 17g; Protein: 2.9g

Butternut Squash Risotto

Serves: 4
Preparation Time: 10 minutes
Cooking Time: 12 minutes
Ingredients:
1 tablespoon vegetable oil
1 white onion, finely chopped
1 red bell pepper, chopped
3 garlic cloves, minced
1½ cups risotto rice
3½ cups of vegetable broth
1 cup chopped button mushrooms
¼ cup white wine
2 cups butternut squash, peeled and diced
3 cups of assorted greens (spinach, kale, and chard)
Salt and pepper to taste
1 tablespoon nutritional yeast

Directions:
1. Heat the vegetable oil in the Instant Pot on SAUTÉ.
2. To this, add minced garlic, onions, and chopped bell pepper, and sauté until they turn slightly soft.
3. Throw in the risotto rice and stir well.
4. Pour the vegetable broth into the pot, followed by the wine, chopped mushrooms, butternut squash, greens, salt, and pepper, and mix well.
5. Cover the lid and cook at high pressure for 7 minutes.
6. When the cooking is complete, do a natural pressure release for 10 minutes. Quick release the remaining pressure.
7. Transfer the risotto to the bowls. Sprinkle nutritional yeast on top and stir. The mixture will thicken shortly, and be ready to serve.

Nutritional Information (Per Serving)
Calories: 412; Fat: 5.6g; Net Carbohydrates: 68.9g; Protein: 13.2g

Spinach with Tomatoes

Serves: 4
Preparation Time: 15 minutes
Cooking Time: 12 minutes
Ingredients:
2 tablespoons olive oil
2 small onions, chopped
2 teaspoons garlic, minced
10 cups fresh spinach, chopped
1 cup tomatoes, chopped
½ cup tomato puree
1½ cups vegetable broth
1 tablespoon fresh lemon juice
½ teaspoon red pepper flakes, crushed
Salt and pepper to taste

Directions:
1. Place the oil in the Instant Pot and select SAUTÉ. Add the onion and cook for about 3 minutes.
2. Add the garlic and red pepper flakes and cook for 1 minute.
3. Add spinach and cook for 2 minutes.
4. Press the CANCEL button and stir in the remaining ingredients.
5. Secure the lid and cook at high pressure for 6 minutes.
6. When the cooking is complete, carefully do a quick pressure release.
7. Serve warm.

Nutritional Information (Per Serving)
Calories: 129; Fat: 8.1g; Net Carbohydrates: 7.9g; Protein: 5.4g

Cherry Tomato Cacciatore

Serves: 4
Preparation Time: 10 minutes
Cooking Time: 19 minutes
Ingredients:
1 tablespoon olive oil
2 cups fresh cherry tomatoes
3 pounds chicken thighs
2 garlic cloves, minced
¾ teaspoon chili flakes
1 teaspoon sea salt
1 teaspoon oregano
3 tablespoons red wine
1 cup water
Some fresh basil leaves
½ cup olives, chopped

Directions:
1. Add the oil to an Instant Pot and set to SAUTÉ.
2. Slide in the chicken thighs and cook until brown on all sides. Set the chicken aside in a large bowl.
3. Put the cherry tomatoes in a Ziplock bag and pound them gently with a pounder.
4. Mix the cherry tomatoes with the browned chicken in the bowl. To this, add minced garlic cloves, chili flakes, sea salt, oregano, red wine, and water and mix well.
5. Transfer this mix to the Instant Pot and cook for 13–14 minutes at high pressure.
6. When the cooking is complete, use a natural pressure release.
7. Serve with some basil leaves and chopped olives on top.

Nutritional Information (Per Serving)
Calories: 725; Fat: 30.7g; Net Carbohydrates: 3.8g; Protein: 99.5g

Black Beans and Burrito Bowl

Serves: 6
Preparation Time: 15 minutes
Cooking Time: 17 minutes
Ingredients:
1 tablespoon olive oil
1 pound chicken breast (boneless)
1 large red onion, finely chopped
1 large yellow bell pepper, chopped
1 cup black beans, soaked for at least 4 hours
1 cup water
1 teaspoon sea salt
1 teaspoon cayenne pepper
1 bay leaf
1 teaspoon garlic powder
Cumin powder to taste
1 cup lettuce

For the rice
1½ cups rice
1½ cups water
1 tablespoon lemon juice

Directions:
1. Rinse the rice with water. In a large bowl (heatproof), add the rice, water, and lemon juice. Set it aside.
2. Heat the olive oil in the Instant Pot and set it to SAUTÉ. Lay the chicken pieces in it and cook until brown on both sides. Set it aside on a plate.
3. Add the onion, black beans, salt, pepper, garlic powder, cumin powder, bay leaf, and water to the Instant Pot and mix well.
4. Lay the browned chicken pieces on top of this mixture.
5. Set the rice bowl into a steamer basket. Lower the basket to the pot.
6. Cover the lid and cook at high pressure for 12 minutes.

7. When the cooking is complete, do a natural pressure release for 10 minutes. Quick release the remaining pressure.

8. Make burritos by layering the bean mixture, rice, and lettuce leaves.

Nutritional Information (Per Serving)
Calories: 406; Fat: 5.2g; Net Carbohydrates: 55.3g; Protein: 27g

Cabbage with Carrot

Serves: 4
Preparation Time: 20 minutes
Cooking Time: 10 minutes
Ingredients:
2 tablespoons coconut oil
2 small onions, sliced
Salt to taste
2 garlic cloves, chopped
1 jalapeño pepper, seeded and chopped
1 tablespoon mild curry powder
1 medium head cabbage, shredded
2 small carrots, peeled and sliced
½ cup desiccated unsweetened coconut
2 tablespoons fresh lemon juice
1 cup water

Directions:
1. Place the coconut oil in the Instant Pot and select SAUTÉ. Add the onion and salt and cook for 4 minutes.

2. Add the garlic, jalapeño, and curry powder and cook for 1 minute.

3. Press CANCEL and stir in the remaining ingredients.

4. Secure the lid and cook at high pressure for 5 minutes.

5. When the cooking is complete, do a natural pressure release for 5 minutes. Quick release the remaining pressure.

6. Serve warm.

Nutritional Information (Per Serving)
Calories: 185; Fat: 10.7g; Net Carbohydrates: 13.6g; Protein: 4.3g

Garlic Mashed Potatoes

Serves: 4
Preparation Time: 5 minutes
Cooking Time: 5 minutes
Ingredients:
4 medium russet potatoes
1 cup vegetable broth
6 garlic cloves, minced
4 tablespoons parsley, chopped
Salt to taste
½ cup low-fat milk

Directions:
1. Cut the potatoes into medium-sized chunks.
2. Put the chunks into the Instant Pot along with the garlic and broth.
3. Close the lid and cook at high pressure for 5 minutes.
4. When the cooking is complete, do a natural pressure release.
5. Open the lid carefully and with a handheld masher, mash the potato.
6. Add milk, parsley, and salt and stir well to combine.
7. Serve hot.

Nutritional Information (Per Serving)
Calories: 177; Fat: 0.9g; Net Carbohydrates: 31.6g; Protein: 6.2g

Vegetable Curry

Serves: 6
Preparation Time: 15 minutes
Cooking Time: 25 minutes
Ingredients:

2 tablespoons coconut oil
1 large onion, finely chopped
3 cloves garlic, minced
2 tablespoons curry powder
1 teaspoon turmeric powder
1 can (14 ounces) diced tomatoes
1 can (14 ounces) coconut milk
2 medium potatoes, diced
2 carrots, sliced
1 cup green beans, cut into 1-inch pieces
1 bell pepper, chopped
1 cup cauliflower florets
1 cup peas
Salt and pepper to taste

Directions:

1. Set your Instant Pot to SAUTÉ and add the coconut oil.
2. Add the onion and sauté until it becomes translucent. Add the garlic and sauté for another minute.
3. Add curry powder and turmeric powder, and give it a quick stir.
4. Mix in the diced tomatoes and allow it to cook for 2–3 minutes.
5. Add potatoes, carrots, green beans, bell pepper, cauliflower, and peas. Stir well.
6. Pour in the coconut milk and mix well.
7. Close the lid, select the MANUAL or PRESSURE COOK setting, and cook at high pressure for 8 minutes.
8. When the cooking is complete, do a natural pressure release for 10 minutes. Quick release the remaining pressure.

9. Open the lid carefully. Stir the curry and season with salt and pepper.

10. Serve hot.

Nutritional Information (Per Serving)
Calories: 258; Fat: 16.5g; Net Carbohydrates: 21.2g; Protein: 5g

Pumpkin Curry

Serves: 4
Preparation Time: 15 minutes
Cooking Time: 8 minutes
Ingredients:
1 tablespoon coconut oil
1 small onion, chopped
½ tablespoon garlic, minced
½ tablespoon fresh ginger, minced
1 serrano pepper, halved
½ teaspoon cumin seeds
4 cups pumpkin, peeled and chopped
1 tomato, chopped
2 teaspoons ground coriander
¼ teaspoon red chili powder
¼ teaspoon ground turmeric
Salt to taste
¼ cup water

Directions:
1. Place the coconut oil in the Instant Pot and select SAUTÉ. Add the onion, garlic, ginger, serrano pepper, and cumin and cook for 2–3 minutes.

2. Press CANCEL and stir in the remaining ingredients.

3. Close the lid, select the MANUAL or PRESSURE COOK setting, and cook at high pressure for 5 minutes.

4. When the cooking is complete, do a quick pressure release.

5. Serve hot.

Nutritional Information (Per Serving)
Calories: 129; Fat: 4.3g; Net Carbohydrates: 15.3g; Protein: 3.3g

Spinach with Cheese

Serves: 4
Preparation Time: 15 minutes
Cooking Time: 10 minutes
Ingredients:
1 tablespoon butter
1 small yellow onion, chopped
4 garlic cloves, chopped
1 Serrano pepper, chopped
½ teaspoon ground cumin
¼ teaspoon ground coriander
1 tomato, chopped
10 ounces fresh spinach
Salt and pepper to taste
10 ounces cottage cheese, cubed
2 tablespoons cream

Directions:
1. Place the butter in the Instant Pot and select SAUTÉ. Add the onion, garlic, green chili, and spices and cook for 3–4 minutes.
2. Add the tomato and cook for about 2 minutes.
3. Press CANCEL and stir in spinach, salt, and pepper.
4. Close the lid, select the MANUAL or PRESSURE COOK setting, and cook at high pressure for 2 minutes.
5. When the cooking is complete, use a natural pressure release.
6. Remove the lid and with an immerse blender, puree the spinach mixture.
7. Select SAUTÉ and stir in cottage cheese. Cook for about 2 minutes.

8. Transfer the spinach mixture onto serving plates.
9. Top with cream and serve.

Nutritional Information (Per Serving)
Calories: 125; Fat: 5g; Net Carbohydrates: 5.7g; Protein: 12.5g

Tomato with Tofu

Serves: 4
Preparation Time: 10 minutes
Cooking Time: 4 minutes
Ingredients:
1 cup diced tomatoes
1 block firm tofu, cubed
½ cup vegetable broth
2 teaspoons Italian seasoning
2 tablespoons jarred banana pepper rings
1 tablespoon olive oil

Directions:
1. Place all of the ingredients in the Instant Pot. Stir to combine the mixture well.
2. Close the lid, select the MANUAL or PRESSURE COOK setting, and cook at high pressure for 4 minutes.
3. When the cooking is complete, do a quick pressure release.
4. Serve warm.

Nutritional Information (Per Serving)
Calories: 68; Fat: 5.4g; Net Carbohydrates: 2.3g; Protein: 2.9g

CHAPTER SEVEN

Soups, Stews, and Chilis

Beef Stew

Serves: 6
Preparation Time: 10 minutes
Cooking Time: 40 minutes
Ingredients:
1½ pounds stew meat
1 onion, chopped
2 pounds red potatoes, diced
1 cup carrots, sliced
2 cups beef broth
1 tablespoon olive oil
Salt and pepper to taste
1 bay leaf
1 teaspoon garlic powder
2 tablespoons tomato paste
2 tablespoons white flour

Directions:
1. Set the Instant Pot to SAUTÉ. Heat the olive oil and add the stew meat. Sauté the meat until browned.
2. Add the rest of the vegetables and stir.
3. Pour in the broth, add the seasoning, and stir.
4. Shut the lid and press MEAT. Cook at high pressure for 35 minutes.
5. When the cooking is complete, do a quick pressure release.
6. Use a ladle to retrieve half a cup of broth from the Instant Pot and pour it into a small bowl. Mix in the flour to create a slurry.
7. Pour the slurry into the Instant Pot and stir.
8. Adjust the seasoning and serve.

Nutritional Information (Per Serving)
Calories: 454; Fat: 17.9g; Net Carbohydrates: 27.6g; Protein: 40.6g

Chicken Noodle Soup

Serves: 6
Preparation Time: 10 minutes
Cooking Time: 15 minutes
Ingredients:
2 chicken breasts
6 cups chicken stock
2 tablespoons olive oil
3 carrots, chopped
3 celery stalks, chopped
1 cup frozen peas
1 cup frozen corn
2 cups egg noodles
¼ cup fresh parsley
Salt and pepper to taste

Directions:
1. Chop the chicken breast into small, bite-sized pieces and toss with olive oil.
2. Set the Instant Pot to SAUTÉ, add the chicken to brown for about 5 minutes.
3. Add the carrots and celery as well as the salt and pepper. Let everything cook for 2 more minutes.
4. Add the chicken stock, the frozen peas and corn, and the egg noodles. Stir everything together.
5. Seal the Instant Pot lid and cook at high pressure for 8 minutes.
6. When the cooking is complete, do a quick pressure release.
7. Sprinkle with parsley and serve.

Nutritional Information (Per Serving)
Calories: 229; Fat: 7.7g; Net Carbohydrates: 22.4g; Protein: 14.9g

Broccoli Bacon Soup

Serves: 6
Preparation Time: 20 minutes
Cooking Time: 20 minutes
Ingredients:
6 slices of bacon, chopped
1 medium onion, diced
3 cloves garlic, minced
4 cups broccoli florets
4 cups chicken broth
1 cup shredded cheddar cheese
1 cup half-and-half
Salt and pepper to taste

Directions:
1. Set your Instant Pot to SAUTÉ. Add the bacon and cook until crispy, about 4–5 minutes. Remove the bacon and set it aside, leaving the bacon grease in the pot.
2. Add the onion and sauté until it becomes translucent. Add the garlic and sauté for another minute.
3. Add the broccoli florets, salt, pepper, and chicken broth. Stir to combine.
4. Close the lid, choose the MANUAL or PRESSURE COOK setting, and cook at high pressure for 5 minutes.
5. When the cooking is complete, do a natural pressure release for 10 minutes. Quick release the remaining pressure.
6. Open the lid, and blend the mixture with a hand blender, until smooth.
7. Set the Instant Pot to SAUTÉ. Stir in the cheddar cheese and half-and-half. Stir until the cheese is melted.
8. Top with the cooked bacon and serve.

Nutritional Information (Per Serving)
Calories: 182; Fat: 11g; Net Carbohydrates: 8.7g; Protein: 10.3g

Coconut Chicken Soup

Serves: 6
Preparation Time: 20 minutes
Cooking Time: 20 minutes
Ingredients:
1½ pounds boneless, skinless chicken breasts, cubed
2 tablespoons olive oil
1 medium onion, finely chopped
3 cloves garlic, minced
1-inch ginger, grated
1 can (14 ounces) coconut milk
4 cups chicken broth
1 red bell pepper, sliced into thin strips
1 carrot, thinly sliced
2 tablespoons soy sauce
1 tablespoon lime juice
1 teaspoon ground cumin
1 teaspoon red chili flakes
Salt and pepper to taste
¼ cup fresh cilantro, chopped (for garnish)

Directions:
1. Set your Instant Pot to SAUTÉ and add the olive oil.
2. Add the onion and sauté until it becomes translucent. Add the garlic and ginger, and sauté for another minute.
3. Add the chicken pieces to the pot along with ground cumin, red chili flakes, salt, and pepper. Stir and sauté for 3–5 minutes
4. Add the red bell pepper and carrot, and stir to combine.
5. Pour in the chicken broth, coconut milk, and soy sauce. Stir well.

6. Close the lid, choose the MANUAL or PRESSURE COOK setting, and cook at high pressure for 10 minutes.

7. When the cooking is complete, do a natural pressure release for 10 minutes. Quick release the remaining pressure.

8. Garnish with fresh cilantro and serve.

Nutritional Information (Per Serving)
Calories: 301; Fat: 19g; Net Carbohydrates: 7.4g; Protein: 23.6g

Split Pea Soup

Serves: 4
Preparation Time: 10 minutes
Cooking Time: 20 minutes
Ingredients:
1 cup dried split peas
1 cup chicken stock
1 cup water
4 slices Canadian bacon, chopped
1 onion, sliced
2 small red potatoes, chopped
2 cloves garlic, minced
½ cup cream
2 tablespoons fresh parsley
Salt and pepper to taste

Directions:
1. Set the Instant Pot to SAUTÉ. Add bacon and as fat comes off the bacon, stir in the onion and garlic. Cook for 3 minutes.

2. Add the chicken stock, water, and potatoes.

3. Stir in the cream and the peas until everything is combined.

4. Cook for 15 minutes at high pressure.

5. When the cooking is complete, do a natural pressure release.

6. Season with salt and pepper and parsley.

Nutritional Information (Per Serving)
Calories: 366; Fat: 10.5g; Net Carbohydrates: 33.1g; Protein: 21.6g

High Fiber Vegetable Soup

Serves: 6
Preparation Time: 10 minutes
Cooking Time: 10 minutes
Ingredients:
1 tablespoon vegetable oil
4 garlic cloves, minced
1 cup carrots, chopped
1 cup green bell pepper, chopped
1 cup shredded cabbage
1 cup broccoli florets
½ cup kidney beans
¼ cup quinoa
1 teaspoon oregano
1 tablespoon soy sauce
1 teaspoon onion powder
4 cups vegetable broth
¼ teaspoon salt
2 tablespoons lemon juice
Some ground pepper
Some basil leaves

Directions:
1. Set the Instant Pot to SAUTÉ and heat the vegetable oil.
2. Add minced garlic and sauté for about a minute.
3. Add the remaining ingredients to the pot slowly, except for basil leaves and pepper. Stir to mix well.
4. Close the lid and cook at high pressure for 5 minutes.
5. Let the pressure release naturally, and transfer to large soup bowls.
6. Season with some ground pepper and garnish with basil leaves.

Nutritional Information (Per Serving)
Calories: 153; Fat: 4g; Net Carbohydrates: 16.6g; Protein: 9g

Cauliflower Potato Soup

Serves: 6
Preparation Time: 10 minutes
Cooking Time: 10 minutes
Ingredients:
6 slices of raw bacon, chopped
5 garlic cloves, minced
1 medium onion, diced
1 bunch scallions, chopped
Salt and pepper to taste
1 cauliflower, chopped
2 potatoes, diced
4 cups chicken broth
¾ cup heavy cream
1 bay leaf

Directions:
1. Set the Instant Pot on SAUTÉ, add the bacon, and cook for 4 minutes, until crisp.
2. Place bacon on a paper towel. Crumble after excess fat is absorbed.
3. Place the garlic, onion, and scallion in the Instant Pot and cook for 1 minute. Season with salt and pepper.
4. Put some of the broth into the Instant Pot and deglaze the bottom.
5. Add the cauliflower, potatoes, remaining broth, and bay leaf.
6. Shut the lid and cook at high pressure for 5 minutes.
7. When the cooking is complete, do a natural pressure release.
8. Open the lid. Remove the bay leaf.
9. Pour the soup into a large bowl and add the bacon bits and heavy cream.
10. Use a hand blender to achieve a smooth consistency.

Nutritional Information (Per Serving)
Calories: 247; Fat: 14.1g; Net Carbohydrates: 15.8g; Protein: 11.4g

Butternut Squash Soup

Serves: 8
Preparation Time: 10 minutes
Cooking Time: 30 minutes
Ingredients:
6 cups butternut squash, peeled and diced
1 large onion, chopped
3 large carrots, chopped
2 cups celery stalk, chopped
4 garlic cloves, minced
6 cups chicken broth
1 teaspoon cayenne pepper
¼ teaspoon salt
1½ cups coconut milk
2 teaspoons dried oregano
1 teaspoon paprika
Some parsley leaves

Directions:
1. Set the Instant Pot to SAUTÉ. Add the butternut squash, chopped onion, carrots, garlic, and celery.
2. Pour in the chicken broth, and bring this mixture to a boil.
3. Press CANCEL. Close the lid and select SOUP and the default setting.
4. When the cooking is complete, do a natural pressure release.
5. Open the lid and let the mixture cool down.
6. Using a hand blender, blend all ingredients into a fine paste.
7. Set the Instant Pot to SAUTÉ. Add oregano, coconut milk, cayenne pepper, paprika, and salt. Let it simmer for 5 minutes.
8. Garnish with fresh parsley and serve.

Nutritional Information (Per Serving)
Calories: 483; Fat: 40.7g; Net Carbohydrates: 20.8g; Protein: 9.3g

Lentil Soup

Serves: 6
Preparation Time: 15 minutes
Cooking Time: 8 minutes
Ingredients:
2 cups lentils
3 garlic cloves, minced
1 onion, diced
1 tablespoon olive oil
2 teaspoons cumin
1 teaspoon paprika
2 carrots, sliced
2 celery stalks, sliced
1 pound Yukon potatoes
2 cups spinach, chopped
6 cups water
Salt and pepper to taste

Directions:
1. Set the Instant Pot to SAUTÉ and add the olive oil. Sauté the garlic, onions, cumin, paprika, celery, and potatoes for 5 minutes.
2. Add the lentils and stir.
3. Cover the ingredients with water.
4. Lock the lid and cook for 3 minutes at high pressure.
5. When the cooking is complete, use a quick pressure release.
6. Mix in the spinach and adjust the seasoning.

Nutritional Information (Per Serving)
Calories: 336; Fat: 3.4g; Net Carbohydrates: 36.5g; Protein: 18.8g

Creamy Tomato Soup

Serves: 4
Preparation Time: 5 minutes
Cooking Time: 5 minutes
Ingredients:
6 large tomatoes
1 cup water
1 cup heavy cream
½ cup fresh basil leaves, chopped
1 tablespoon dried oregano
½ teaspoon salt
1 teaspoon white pepper

Directions:
1. Cut the tomatoes into halves and place them in the Instant Pot.
2. Add one cup of water. Cook at high pressure for 5 minutes and allow pressure to release naturally.
3. Remove the lid and use a hand blender to achieve a smooth consistency.
4. Add the cream, herbs, salt, and pepper to taste.

Nutritional Information (Per Serving)
Calories: 158; Fat: 11.8g; Net Carbohydrates: 8.6g; Protein: 3.3g

Hot and Sour Soup

Serves: 4
Preparation Time: 10 minutes
Cooking Time: 15 minutes
Ingredients:
½ pound chicken breast, cubed
1 tablespoon sesame oil
2 cups chicken stock
1 cup water
2 tablespoons fresh ginger, grated
1 tablespoon freshly squeezed lime juice
1 whole chili pepper, sliced and seeded
1 tomato, chopped
½ cup fresh mushrooms, sliced
1 tablespoon fish sauce
2 tablespoons fresh cilantro

Directions:
1. Set the Instant Pot to SAUTÉ. Toss the chicken pieces in the sesame oil and heat in the Instant Pot for 5 minutes.
2. Add the chicken stock, water, ginger, lime juice, chili pepper, tomato, and mushrooms. Stir together. Press CANCEL.
3. Close the lid, choose the MANUAL or PRESSURE COOK setting, and cook at high pressure for 10 minutes.
4. When the cooking is complete, do a natural pressure release.
5. Stir in the fish sauce and the cilantro, and serve.

Nutritional Information (Per Serving)
Calories: 118; Fat: 5.3g; Net Carbohydrates: 3.4g; Protein: 13.3g

Ham and Bean Soup

Serves: 6
Preparation Time: 10 minutes
Cooking Time: 25 minutes
Ingredients:
1 pound dried black beans
2 cups water
2 cups tomatoes, diced
1 small onion, chopped
1 cup frozen peas
1 clove garlic
2 cups cooked ham, cubed

Directions:
1. Put the dried beans in the Instant Pot and cover with water and tomatoes.
2. Add the onion, peas, and garlic.
3. Cook at high pressure for 25 minutes and allow the pressure to ease naturally.
4. Open the pot and stir in the cubed ham.

Nutritional Information (Per Serving)
Calories: 368; Fat: 5.1g; Net Carbohydrates: 41.8g; Protein: 25.9g

Minestrone Soup

Serves: 8
Preparation Time: 15 minutes
Cooking Time: 11 minutes
Ingredients:
2 tablespoons olive oil
2 stalks celery, diced
1 large onion, diced
3 cloves garlic, minced
1 carrot, diced
1 teaspoon oregano
1 teaspoon basil
Salt and pepper to taste
28 ounces tomatoes, diced
4 cups vegetable broth
1 cup elbow pasta
1 bay leaf
2 cups canned cannellini beans
½ cup spinach, chopped
½ cup grated parmesan cheese

Directions:
1. Set the Instant Pot to SAUTÉ.
2. Sauté the onion, carrot, celery, and garlic in the olive oil for 5 minutes. Top with salt, pepper, oregano, basil, diced tomatoes, bay leaf, broth, and pasta. Press CANCEL.
3. Close the lid, choose the MANUAL or PRESSURE COOK setting, and cook at high pressure for 6 minutes.
4. After the cooking is complete, let the soup sit for a few minutes. Do a quick pressure release.
5. Open the lid and add the white beans and the spinach. Stir well.
6. Garnish with the parmesan cheese and serve.

Nutritional Information (Per Serving)
Calories: 384; Fat: 8.6g; Net Carbohydrates: 42.1g; Protein: 23.1g

Beef Barley Soup

Serves: 6
Preparation Time: 10 minutes
Cooking Time: 20 minutes
Ingredients:
8 cups beef stock
¾ cup pearl barley
1 pound sliced Bella mushrooms
1 onion, diced
2 carrots, diced
2 celery stalks, diced
3 garlic cloves, minced
3 thyme sprigs
¼ teaspoon garlic powder
Salt and pepper to taste

Directions:
1. Combine all of the ingredients in an Instant Pot.
2. Cover the lid, choose the MANUAL or PRESSURE COOK setting, and cook at high pressure for 20 minutes.
3. Allow the pressure to release naturally for 10 minutes. Quick release the remaining pressure.
4. Serve hot.

Nutritional Information (Per Serving)
Calories: 148; Fat: 1g; Net Carbohydrates: 20.4g; Protein: 9.3g

Oxtail Soup

Serves: 6
Preparation Time: 15 minutes
Cooking Time: 45 minutes
Ingredients:
2 pounds oxtail, chopped into bite-sized pieces
2 tomatoes, diced
2 celery stalks, diced
2 carrots, diced
1 scallion, sliced
1 tablespoon vegetable oil
2 tablespoons tomato paste
Salt and pepper to taste
3 ginger slices, finely minced
½ cup white wine
5 cups water

Directions:
1. Place all of the ingredients in an Instant Pot.
2. Close the lid, and cook at high pressure for 45 minutes.
3. Let the pressure release naturally.
4. Serve hot.

Nutritional Information (Per Serving)
Calories: 255; Fat: 14.8g; Net Carbohydrates: 4.3g; Protein: 20.6g

Chicken and Salsa Soup

Serves: 6
Preparation Time: 15 minutes
Cooking Time: 17 minutes
Ingredients:
2 pounds boneless, skinless chicken breasts
1 (15-ounce) jar salsa
2 Serrano peppers, chopped
2 tablespoons ground cumin
1 tablespoon red chili powder
Freshly ground black pepper to taste
5 cups chicken broth
1 cup water
1 (8-ounce) block cream cheese, softened and chopped

Directions:
1. In the Instant Pot, add all ingredients except for cream cheese and stir to combine.
2. Close the lid, select the MANUAL or PRESSURE COOK setting, and cook at high pressure for 15 minutes.
3. When the cooking is complete, do a natural pressure release for 10 minutes. Quick release the remaining pressure.
4. Remove the lid and with a slotted spoon, transfer the chicken breasts into a bowl.
5. With 2 forks, shred chicken breasts and then return to the pot.
6. Select SAUTÉ and stir in cream cheese. Cook for 1–2 minutes, stirring continuously.
7. Serve hot.

Nutritional Information (Per Serving)
Calories: 463; Fat: 25.2g; Net Carbohydrates: 6.1g; Protein: 49.9g

Lamb Stew

Serves: 6
Preparation Time: 15 minutes
Cooking Time: 45 minutes
Ingredients:
2 pounds lamb shoulder, cubed
2 tablespoons olive oil
1 large onion, chopped
3 garlic cloves, minced
3 large carrots, cut into 1-inch pieces
3 potatoes, peeled and cut into 1.5-inch cubes
3 cups beef broth
2 teaspoons salt
½ teaspoon black pepper
1 teaspoon dried thyme
2 tablespoons tomato paste
Fresh parsley, finely chopped (for garnish)

Directions:
1. Set your Instant Pot to SAUTÉ and add the olive oil.
2. Add lamb cubes. Brown the lamb on all sides (you may need to do this in batches). Remove the lamb and set aside.
3. In the same pot, add the onion and sauté until translucent. Add the garlic and sauté for another minute.
4. Return the browned lamb to the pot. Add the remaining ingredients except for the fresh parsley.
5. Close the lid and press MEAT. Cook at high pressure for 35 minutes.
6. When the cooking is complete, do a natural pressure release for 10 minutes. Quick release the remaining pressure.
7. Garnish with fresh parsley and serve.

Nutritional Information (Per Serving)
Calories: 383; Fat: 20.5g; Net Carbohydrates: 23.8g; Protein: 25.4g

Mushroom Stew

Serves: 6
Preparation Time: 15 minutes
Cooking Time: 20 minutes
Ingredients:
2 tablespoons olive oil
1 medium onion, finely chopped
4 cloves garlic, minced
1 pound mushrooms, sliced
3 medium carrots, sliced
2 medium potatoes, cubed
Salt to taste
½ teaspoon black pepper
½ teaspoon dried thyme
½ teaspoon dried rosemary
4 cups vegetable broth

Directions:
1. Set your Instant Pot to SAUTÉ and add the olive oil.
2. Add the onion and sauté until it becomes translucent. Add the garlic and sauté for another minute.
3. Add the mushrooms and sauté for 3–5 minutes until they start to soften.
4. Add the rest ingredients and stir to combine.
5. Close the lid, choose the MANUAL or PRESSURE COOK setting, and cook at high pressure for 10 minutes.
6. When the cooking is complete, do a natural pressure release for 10 minutes. Quick release the remaining pressure.
7. Serve hot.

Nutritional Information (Per Serving)
Calories: 141; Fat: 4.7g; Net Carbohydrates: 21g; Protein: 4.1g

Beef & Pork Chili

Serves: 8
Preparation Time: 15 minutes
Cooking Time: 35 minutes
Ingredients:
1 tablespoon olive oil
1 pound ground beef
1 pound ground pork
3 medium tomatillos, chopped
1 yellow onion, chopped
2 jalapeño peppers, chopped
2 garlic cloves, minced
6 ounces homemade tomato sauce
1 tablespoon red chili powder
1 tablespoon ground cumin
Salt and pepper to taste
¼ cup water

Directions:

1. Place the oil in the Instant Pot and select SAUTÉ. Then add the beef and pork and cook for about 5 minutes.

2. Remove extra grease from the pot.

3. Stir in the remaining ingredients.

4. Close the lid, select the MANUAL or PRESSURE COOK setting, and cook at high pressure for 35 minutes.

5. When the cooking is complete, use a natural pressure release.

6. Serve hot.

Nutritional Information (Per Serving)
Calories: 227; Fat: 10.6g; Net Carbohydrates: 3g; Protein: 7.2g

Turkey Chili

Serves: 8
Preparation Time: 15 minutes
Cooking Time: 35 minutes
Ingredients:
1 tablespoon olive oil
1 red bell pepper, seeded and chopped
1 yellow onion, chopped
3 garlic cloves, minced
2 pounds ground turkey
2¼ cups tomatoes, chopped finely
1 (4-ounce) can fire-roasted diced green chilis
¾ cup homemade pumpkin puree
3 tablespoons red chili powder
1 tablespoon paprika
1 teaspoon cayenne pepper
1½ tablespoons ground cumin
1 tablespoon pumpkin pie spice
1 tablespoon dried oregano
Salt to taste
½ cup homemade chicken broth

Directions:
1. Place the oil in the Instant Pot and select SAUTÉ. Add the bell pepper, onion, and garlic and cook for 4–5 minutes.
2. Ad turkey and cook for about 5 minutes.
3. Stir in the remaining ingredients.
4. Close the lid, select the MANUAL or PRESSURE COOK setting, and cook at high pressure for 20 minutes.
5. When the cooking is complete, use a natural pressure release.
6. Serve hot.

Nutritional Information (Per Serving)
Calories: 346; Fat: 16.5g; Net Carbohydrates: 14.2g; Protein: 35.3g

CHAPTER EIGHT

Snacks and Appetizers

Cheesy Spinach Dip

Serves: 6
Preparation Time: 5 minutes
Cooking Time: 10 minutes
Ingredients:
6 ounces frozen spinach, chopped
½ teaspoon thyme
¼ teaspoon garlic salt
2 tablespoons Parmesan cheese
8 ounces cream cheese
1 teaspoon Worcestershire sauce
¼ cup Whipping cream

Directions:
1. Use a baking dish that will fit into your Instant Pot. Butter the inside of the dish.
2. Add all the ingredients to the dish and mix to combine. Cover the dish with aluminum foil.
3. Fill the Instant Pot with a cup of water.
4. Place a trivet in the Instant Pot, and place the dish on the trivet.
5. Close the lid, choose the MANUAL or PRESSURE COOK setting, and cook at high pressure for 10 minutes.
6. When the cooking is complete, do a quick pressure release.
7. Serve with crackers.

Nutritional Information (Per Serving)
Calories: 158; Fat: 15.1g; Net Carbohydrates: 1.8g; Protein: 4.2g

Jalapeño Poppers

Serves: 6
Preparation Time: 20 minutes
Cooking Time: 10 minutes
Ingredients:
6 large jalapeños, halved lengthwise and seeds removed
8 ounces cream cheese, softened
1 cup cheddar cheese, shredded
½ teaspoon garlic powder
½ teaspoon onion powder
Salt to taste
1 cup water

Directions:
1. In a bowl, combine the cream cheese, cheddar cheese, garlic powder, onion powder, and salt.
2. Using a spoon, stuff each jalapeño half with the cheese mixture.
3. Place a trivet inside the Instant Pot and fill with 1 cup of water.
4. Arrange the stuffed jalapeño halves on the trivet, cheese side up.
5. Cover the lid, choose the MANUAL or PRESSURE COOK setting, and cook at high pressure for 8 minutes
6. When the cooking is complete, carefully do a quick pressure release.
7. Serve hot.

Nutritional Information (Per Serving)
Calories: 226; Fat: 21g; Net Carbohydrates: 3.4g; Protein: 7g

Carrot Sticks

Serves: 4
Preparation Time: 15 minutes
Cooking Time: 10 minutes
Ingredients:
1 pound carrots
2 tablespoons butter
2 tablespoons honey
2 tablespoons Dijon mustard
2 teaspoons garlic, minced
1 teaspoon ground cumin
½ teaspoon paprika
Salt and pepper to taste
Dash of hot sauce

Directions:
1. Cut the carrots into quarters lengthwise and then cut each quarter in half.
2. Arrange a steamer trivet in the Instant Pot. Add 1 cup of water to the Instant Pot.
3. Arrange the carrots on top of the trivet.
4. Secure the lid and cook at high pressure for 2 minutes.
5. When the cooking is complete, do a quick pressure release.
6. Remove the lid and transfer the carrots onto a plate.
7. Remove the steamer basket and all water from the pot and with paper towels, pat the pot dry.
8. Place the butter in the Instant Pot and select SAUTÉ. Add the remaining ingredients and stir to combine.
9. Press CANCEL and stir in the carrots.
10. Serve warm.

Nutritional Information (Per Serving)
Calories: 140; Fat: 6.2g; Net Carbohydrates: 17.8g; Protein: 1.6g

Hot Chicken Wings

Serves: 6
Preparation Time: 15 minutes
Cooking Time: 10 minutes
Ingredients:
6 chicken wings, drumettes and flats separated
1 cup water
1 teaspoon salt
½ teaspoon black pepper

For Hot Sauce:
½ cup hot sauce
¼ cup unsalted butter
1 teaspoon garlic powder
½ teaspoon onion powder
Salt to taste

Directions:
1. Season the wings with salt and black pepper.
2. Place a trivet inside the Instant Pot and fill with 1 cup of water.
3. Place the chicken wings on the trivet.
4. Cover the lid, choose the MANUAL or PRESSURE COOK setting, and cook at high pressure for 8 minutes
5. When the cooking is complete, carefully do a quick pressure release.
6. While the chicken is cooking, make the hot sauce. In a saucepan, melt the butter over low heat. Add the hot sauce, garlic powder, onion powder, and salt. Stir until well combined. Remove from heat and set aside.
7. Carefully remove the wings from the Instant Pot and place them in a large bowl. Pour the hot sauce over the wings and toss until they are well coated.
8. Serve immediately.

Nutritional Information (Per Serving)

Calories: 82; Fat: 7g; Net Carbohydrates: 1.4g; Protein: 4g

Creamy Artichoke Dip

Serves: 6
Preparation Time: 10 minutes
Cooking Time: 60 minutes
Ingredients:
½ cup cannellini beans, soaked for about 4 hours
1 cup vegetable broth
8 medium-sized artichokes
2 garlic cloves, minced
½ lemon
¾ cup plain yogurt
¾ teaspoon salt
¼ teaspoon ground pepper
½ cup grated ricotta cheese
Some nachos

Directions:
1. Wash the artichokes under running water and slice them into halves.
2. Boil artichokes in water for 30 minutes. Remove the leaves and carefully remove the chokes using a spoon.
3. Add the artichokes to an Instant Pot. Add the minced garlic cloves, lemon, vegetable broth, and beans and mix well.
4. Cook this mixture for 20 minutes at high pressure.
5. When the cooking is complete, use a natural pressure release.
6. Open the lid and let the mixture stand for a few minutes.
7. Add yogurt, ground pepper, salt, and cheese and mix well.
8. Transfer to a blender and combine until it forms a smooth paste.
9. Serve along with some nachos.

Nutritional Information (Per Serving)

Calories: 191; Fat: 2.6g; Net Carbohydrates: 18.2g; Protein: 14.2g

Cheese Broccoli Dip

Serves: 8
Preparation Time: 10 minutes
Cooking Time: 4 minutes
Ingredients:
1 pound Velveeta cheese, cubed
1 cup cheddar cheese, shredded
1 cup mozzarella cheese, shredded
1 cup broccoli florets, finely chopped
1 can (10 ounces) diced tomatoes, drained
½ cup whole milk
½ cup sour cream
1 teaspoon garlic powder
½ teaspoon onion powder
Salt and pepper to taste

Directions:
1. Combine all of the ingredients in your Instant Pot.
2. Cover the lid, choose the MANUAL or PRESSURE COOK setting, and cook at high pressure for 4 minutes.
3. Allow the pressure to release naturally for 10 minutes. Quick release the remaining pressure.
4. Open the lid and stir the mixture with a wooden spoon until smooth.
5. Serve warm with tortilla chips or sliced baguette.

Nutritional Information (Per Serving)
Calories: 267; Fat: 17.4g; Net Carbohydrates: 11.1g; Protein: 13.9g

Candied Lemon Peels

Yield: about 80 strips
Preparation Time: 20 minutes
Cooking Time: 10 minutes
Ingredients:
1 pound lemons
3 cups brown sugar, divided
4 cups of water

Directions:

1. Wash the lemons thoroughly and pat them dry with a paper towel.

2. Slice the lemons in half. Scoop out the pulp using a sharp knife.

3. Cut the lemon peel into thin strips. Add the peels to the Instant Pot, followed by 3 cups of brown sugar and the water.

4. Cover the lid and cook for 10 minutes at high pressure.

5. When the cooking is complete, do a quick pressure release.

6. Drain the peels, lay them on a sheet, sprinkle some sugar on top and refrigerate overnight. Store in an airtight container for up to 6 weeks.

Nutritional Information (Per Strip)
Calories: 22.5; Fat: 0g; Net Carbohydrates: 5.7g; Protein: 0.1g

Tangy Sweet Potato Wedges

Serves: 4
Preparation Time: 10 minutes
Cooking Time: 20 minutes
Ingredients:
3 large sweet potatoes
½ teaspoon salt
1 tablespoon dry mango powder
1 teaspoon paprika
2 tablespoons vegetable oil
1 cup water

Directions:
1. Wash the sweet potatoes thoroughly and peel them. Cut into medium-sized wedges.
2. Add 1 cup water and place a trivet in the Instant Pot.
3. Lay the sweet potato wedges on it and cook for 15 minutes at high pressure.
4. When the cooking is complete, do a quick pressure release.
5. Remove and place the wedges on a plate.
6. Heat the vegetable oil in a saucepan over medium-high heat. Slide in the sweet potato wedges and pan-sear until they turn brown.
7. Combine dry mango powder, salt, and paprika in a bowl and mix well.
8. Coat the wedges generously with this mixture and serve.

Nutritional Information (Per Serving)
Calories: 162; Fat: 6.9g; Net Carbohydrates: 22.6g; Protein: 1.6g

Prosciutto Wrapped Asparagus

Serves: 4
Preparation Time: 15 minutes
Cooking Time: 3 minutes
Ingredients:
1 pound asparagus spears
10 ounces prosciutto, sliced

Directions:
1. Wrap the prosciutto slices around the asparagus spears.
2. Arrange a steamer basket in the Instant Pot. Add 2 cups of water to the Instant Pot.
3. Arrange any extra un-wrapped spears in the bottom of the steamer basket in a single layer.
4. Place prosciutto-wrapped asparagus on top in a single layer.
5. Secure the lid and cook at high pressure for 2–3 minutes.
6. When the cooking is complete, do a natural pressure release.
7. Serve warm.

Nutritional Information (Per Serving)
Calories: 125; Fat: 4.1g; Net Carbohydrates: 3.1g; Protein: 17.3g

Scotch Eggs

Serves: 4
Preparation Time: 5 minutes
Cooking Time: 20 minutes
Ingredients:
4 large eggs
1 pound ground sausage meat
1 tablespoon vegetable oil

Directions:
1. Add the steamer basket to the Instant Pot.
2. Pour in a cup of water and add the eggs.
3. Lock the Instant Pot lid. Cook at high pressure for 6 minutes.
4. When the cooking is complete, do a natural pressure release for 6 minutes. Quick release the remaining pressure.
5. Open the pot and carefully lift the steamer basket from the pot.
6. Let the eggs cool in cold water. Peel the eggs.
7. Divide the pork sausage into 4 portions. Flatten each portion with a kitchen dough roller.
8. Place a hard-boiled egg in the center of each sausage piece. Wrap each egg with the flattened sausage.
9. Heat the Instant Pot with the SAUTÉ setting. Add the oil and sauté the Scotch Eggs on each side.
10. Remove the eggs from the Instant Pot.
11. Pour a cup of water into the Instant Pot and place a rack inside. Place the eggs on top of the rack.
12. Lock the Instant Pot lid and cook at high pressure for 6 minutes.
13. When the cooking is complete, do a quick pressure release.

Nutritional Information (Per Serving)
Calories: 334; Fat: 24.6g; Net Carbohydrates: 0.4g; Protein: 26.5g

Chunky Applesauce

Serves: 6
Preparation Time: 10 minutes
Cooking Time: 5 minutes
Ingredients:
10 apples, cored, peeled, and cut into chunks
¼ cup apple juice
¼ cup water
¼ cup sugar
2 teaspoons ground cinnamon

Directions:
1. Place the apples, liquid, sugar, and cinnamon in your Instant Pot.
2. Close the lid and cook for 5 minutes at high pressure.
3. When the cooking is complete, use a natural pressure release.
4. Stir until apples break down to the level of consistency you prefer.

Nutritional Information (Per Serving)
Calories: 231; Fat: 0.7g; Net Carbohydrates: 52.1g; Protein: 1g

Glazed Pears

Serves: 4
Preparation Time: 10 minutes
Cooking Time: 10 minutes
Ingredients:
26 ounces grape juice
12 ounces currant jelly
2 tablespoons fresh lemon juice
1 teaspoon fresh lemon zest, grated
4 pears
½ of a vanilla bean
4 peppercorns
2 rosemary sprigs

Directions:
1. In the bottom of the Instant Pot, mix the grape juice, jelly, lemon juice, and zest.
2. Dip each pear in the juice mixture and coat evenly.
3. Wrap each pear in a piece of foil.
4. Add peppercorns, rosemary, and vanilla bean into the juice mixture.
5. Arrange a steamer basket over the juice mixture.
6. Place the pears into the steamer basket.
7. Secure the lid and cook at high pressure for 10 minutes.
8. When the cooking is complete, do a quick pressure release.
9. Transfer the pears onto a platter. Unwrap the pears and arrange them in pudding bowls.
10. Top each pear with the spicy cooking liquid and serve.

Nutritional Information (Per Serving)
Calories: 241; Fat: 0.7g; Net Carbohydrates: 50g; Protein: 3g

Spicy Mushrooms

Serves: 6
Preparation Time: 10 minutes
Cooking Time: 4 minutes
Ingredients:
1 pound white mushrooms, cleaned and halved
1 tablespoon olive oil
½ cup water
4 cloves garlic, minced
1 teaspoon sesame oil
1 teaspoon red pepper flakes
Salt and pepper to taste

Directions:
1. Set your Instant Pot to SAUTÉ and add the olive oil.
2. Add the garlic and sauté until fragrant.
3. Add the rest ingredients to the Instant Pot. Stir to combine.
4. Cover the lid, choose the MANUAL or PRESSURE COOK setting, and cook at high pressure for 4 minutes
5. When the cooking is complete, carefully do a quick pressure release.
6. Serve warm.

Nutritional Information (Per Serving)
Calories: 46; Fat: 2.9g; Net Carbohydrates: 3.3g; Protein: 3g

CHAPTER NINE

Dessert

Coconut Rice Pudding

Serves: 10
Preparation Time: 10 minutes
Cooking Time: 10 minutes
Ingredients:
1 cup uncooked white rice
1½ cups water
2 teaspoons coconut oil
Dash of salt
14 ounces coconut milk
½ cup white sugar
2 large eggs
½ cup milk
1 teaspoon vanilla
Optional: Toasted shredded coconut

Directions:
1. Combine the rice, water, and coconut oil in the Instant Pot.
2. Cook for 5 minutes at high pressure.
3. Use the natural pressure release.
4. Stir in the coconut milk, vanilla, and sugar.
5. In a bowl, whip together eggs and milk. Pour the egg mixture into the Instant Pot while stirring.
6. Press SAUTÉ and stir until the mixture thickens.
7. Pour the rice pudding into individual dishes.
8. Serve warm. You can top with whipped cream and toasted coconut.

Nutritional Information (Per Serving)
Calories: 226; Fat: 11.7g; Net Carbohydrates: 26.6g; Protein: 3.9g

Lemon Coconut Squares

Serves: 12
Preparation Time: 20 minutes
Cooking Time: 30 minutes

Ingredients for the Crust:
1 cup graham cracker crumbs
¼ cup unsweetened shredded coconut
¼ cup granulated sugar
½ stick unsalted butter, melted

Ingredients for the Filling:
1 cup cream cheese, softened
½ cup granulated sugar
2 large eggs
Zest of 1 lemon
2 tablespoons lemon juice
1 teaspoon vanilla extract
¼ cup unsweetened shredded coconut

Directions:
1. Lightly grease a 7-inch springform pan with non-stick spray.
2. In a bowl, combine the graham cracker crumbs, shredded coconut, and sugar. Pour the melted butter over the dry ingredients and mix well.
3. Press this mixture firmly into the bottom of the greased springform pan.
4. Place the pan in the freezer for 10 minutes to firm up the crust.
5. In a large bowl, mix the cream cheese and sugar until smooth.
6. Beat in the eggs one at a time, mixing well.
7. Stir in the lemon zest, lemon juice, vanilla extract, and shredded coconut.
8. Add 1 cup of water into the Instant Pot and place a trivet at the bottom.
9. Take the crust out of the freezer and carefully pour the filling mixture over the crust in the springform pan.

10. Lower the springform pan onto the trivet in the Instant Pot using a foil sling.

11. Close the lid, choose the MANUAL or PRESSURE COOK setting, and cook at high pressure for 25 minutes.

12. When the cooking is complete, do a natural pressure release for 10 minutes. Quick release the remaining pressure.

13. Use the foil sling to lift the cake. Let cool to room temperature.

14. Refrigerate the cheesecake for at least 4 hours. Slice into 12 squares and serve chilled.

Nutritional Information (Per Serving)
Calories: 366; Fat: 16.3g; Net Carbohydrates: 41.1g; Protein: 3g

Chocolate Mousse with Raspberries

Serves: 8
Preparation Time: 10 minutes
Cooking Time: 30 minutes
Ingredients:
1 cup heavy cream
1 cup whole milk
¼ cup super-fine sugar
12 ounces dark cooking chocolate
6 egg yolks
1 teaspoon vanilla extract
2 cups of water
1 tablespoon cocoa powder
6 fresh raspberries

Directions:
1. Stir the cream, milk, and sugar in a saucepan on low heat until the sugar dissolves. Add the chocolate pieces.
2. Whisk the egg yolks until they become thick and slowly add to the chocolate. Add the vanilla.
3. Pour the chocolate mixture into a greased ovenproof dish. Cover with foil.
4. Add the water to the Instant Pot, place the dish on a trivet, and lower the trivet.
5. Close the lid and cook for 20 minutes at high pressure.
6. When the cooking is complete, use a natural pressure release.
7. Once it has cooled, remove the dish. Dust with cocoa powder and place the raspberries in the mousse.

Nutritional Information (Per Serving)
Calories: 372; Fat: 22.7g; Net Carbohydrates: 33.3g; Protein: 6.9g

Green Tea Coconut Crème Brûlée

Serves: 4
Preparation Time: 10 minutes
Cooking Time: 15 minutes
Ingredients:
1 tablespoon green tea powder
1½ cups heavy cream
1 cup coconut milk
1½ teaspoons vanilla extract
¼ teaspoon salt
6 large egg yolks
8 tablespoons brown sugar, divided
Boiling water

Directions:
1. In a large bowl, combine coconut milk, cream, vanilla extract, salt, and mix well.
2. Heat this mixture in a small saucepan while continuously stirring.
3. In another bowl, whisk the egg yolks along with the brown sugar until all ingredients are blended.
4. Pour the cream mixture into the bowl and stir well.
5. Transfer the mixture to small ramekins or heatproof bowls. Be sure to fill only ¾ of the bowl with the mixture, so it leaves room for rising.
6. Add some boiling water to the Instant Pot and set on a trivet. Place the ramekins on it and close the lid. Cook for 5 minutes at high pressure and wait for the pressure to release on its own.
7. Refrigerate the ramekins for at least 4 hours.
8. Remove the ramekins and sprinkle some sugar on top. With the help of a blowtorch, melt the sugar until it turns brown, and serve.

Nutritional Information (Per Serving)
Calories: 461; Fat: 37.7g; Net Carbohydrates: 22.1g; Protein: 6.9g

Pear Applesauce

Makes: 6 cups
Preparation Time: 15 minutes
Cooking Time: 10 minutes
Ingredients:
4 large apples, peeled, cored, and cut into chunks
4 ripe pears, peeled, cored, and cut into chunks
1 cup water
1 teaspoon ground cinnamon
1 tablespoon lemon juice

Directions:
1. Add all ingredients to the Instant Pot. Stir to combine.
2. Close the lid, choose the MANUAL or PRESSURE COOK setting, and cook at high pressure for 8 minutes.
3. When the cooking is complete, do a natural pressure release for 10 minutes. Quick release the remaining pressure.
4. Open the lid, and blend the mixture with a hand blender, until smooth.

Nutritional Information (Per 1 Cup Serving)
Calories: 132; Fat: 0.3g; Net Carbohydrates: 35.2g; Protein: 0.7g

Cranberry Bread Pudding

Serves: 6
Preparation Time: 10 minutes
Cooking Time: 30 minutes
Ingredients:
2 cups milk
4 large beaten eggs
½ cup white sugar
2 teaspoons vanilla
2½ cups old bread, cut into cubes
6 tablespoons raisins
1½ cups water
¼ cup chopped walnuts

Directions:
1. Butter a 1-1/2-quart baking dish.
2. Make an aluminum foil grip: take 2 20x2-inch strips of foil. Crisscross the foil strips and place them in the Instant Pot.
3. In a bowl, combine the milk, eggs, sugar, and vanilla.
4. Add the bread and the raisins to the baking dish. Pour the egg/milk mix on top of the bread cubes. Cover the dish with aluminum foil.
5. Insert a trivet and pour the water into the Instant Pot. Place the dish inside the Instant Pot, making sure the ends of the foil strips are crossed over the dish.
6. Shut the lid and cook at high pressure for 25 minutes.
7. When the cooking is complete, use a natural pressure release.
8. Lift the dish with the foil strips and let cool.
9. Serve warm or cold.
10. If desired, serve with Bourbon Sauce (see recipe below).

Nutritional Information (Per Serving)
Calories: 377; Fat: 10.1g; Net Carbohydrates: 57.6g; Protein: 13.1g

Bourbon Sauce
Ingredients:

¼ cup butter
½ cup sugar
1 egg yolk
2 tablespoons water
3 tablespoons bourbon

Directions:
1. Melt the butter in a saucepan.
2. Remove the pan from the stove and blend in the sugar.
3. Mix in the egg yolk and add the water.
4. Return the pan to the stove and stir until the sauce starts to boil.
5. Remove from the stove and add the bourbon.
6. Serve warm.

Chocolate Pudding

Serves: 6
Preparation Time: 10 minutes
Cooking Time: 18 minutes
Ingredients:
1½ cups whipping cream
½ cup milk
6 ounces bittersweet chocolate slivers
5 egg yolks
¼ cup brown sugar
2 teaspoons vanilla extract
¼ teaspoon cinnamon
Dash of salt

Directions:

1. Heat the whipping cream and milk in a saucepan. Remove from stove and add the chocolate slivers. Stir until the chocolate is melted.

2. In a bowl, combine the remaining ingredients. Stir constantly while adding the hot chocolate.

3. Pour the pudding mix into a baking or soufflé dish and cover with aluminum foil.

4. Insert a trivet in the Instant Pot and pour in 1½ cups water.

5. Place the dish on top of the trivet. Cook at low pressure for 18 minutes.

6. When the cooking is complete, use a natural pressure release.

7. Remove the dish from the Instant Pot and lift the aluminum foil.

8. Cover with Saran wrap and place in refrigerator for 3–4 hours.

9. If desired, garnish with chocolate shavings or crème fraîche.

Nutritional Information (Per Serving)
Calories: 269; Fat: 18.9g; Net Carbohydrates: 18.8g; Protein: 5g

Tapioca Pudding

Serves: 2
Preparation Time: 10 minutes
Cooking Time: 8 minutes
Ingredients:
½ cup tapioca pearls, rinsed
¼ cup raw honey
1¾ cups unsweetened almond milk
¼ teaspoon organic vanilla extract
2 tablespoons almonds, chopped

Directions:
1. In a large heat-proof bowl, add all ingredients except for almonds and stir to combine well.
2. At the bottom of the Instant Pot, arrange a steamer trivet and pour 1 cup of water.
3. Place the bowl on top of the trivet.
4. Close the lid, select the MANUAL or PRESSURE COOK setting, and cook at high pressure for 8 minutes.
5. When the cooking is complete, do a quick pressure release.
6. Let the pudding stand in the Instant Pot for about 5 minutes.
7. Stir to mix the pudding. Serve warm with the topping of almonds.

Nutritional Information (Per Serving)
Calories: 336; Fat: 6g; Net Carbohydrates: 69.7g; Protein: 4.2g

Molten Chocolate Mini Lava Cakes

Serves: 3
Preparation Time: 10 minutes
Cooking Time: 6 minutes
Ingredients:
1 large egg
2 tablespoons olive oil
4 tablespoons all-purpose flour
4 tablespoons milk
4 tablespoons sugar
1 tablespoon cocoa powder
½ teaspoon baking powder
⅛ teaspoon salt
Optional but recommended: ½ teaspoon orange zest

Directions:
1. Grease 3 ramekins with butter.
2. Add 1 cup of water to the Instant Pot and insert a trivet.
3. Use a bowl to mix all ingredients. Blend well.
4. Pour the batter into the ramekins. Leaving a bit of space at the top.
5. Place the ramekins on top of the trivet.
6. Shut the lid and cook at high pressure for 6 minutes for a soft inner cake.
7. When the cooking is complete, use a natural pressure release.

Nutritional Information (Per Serving)
Calories: 217; Fat: 11.8g; Net Carbohydrates: 25.7g; Protein: 4.2g

Chocolate Cake with Jam

Serves: 8
Preparation Time: 10 minutes
Cooking Time: 30 minutes
Ingredients:
1½ cups flour
4 tablespoons cocoa powder
¼ cup blackberry jam
1 cup milk
1 tablespoon salted butter, melted
¾ cup sugar
2 eggs
1 teaspoon baking powder
2 tablespoons confectioner's sugar

Directions:
1. In a bowl, sift together flour, cocoa powder, and baking powder.
2. In a separate bowl, whisk the eggs with the sugar and the melted butter. Stir in the jam until the ingredients are combined.
3. Slowly combine the flour mixture with the wet mixture. Add milk. Pour into a greased pan and place it into the Instant Pot on a trivet.
4. Add 1 cup water to the pot. Close the lid and cook at high pressure for 30 minutes.
5. When the cooking is complete, do a natural pressure release for 10 minutes. Quick release the remaining pressure.
6. Sprinkle with the confectioner's sugar once the cake has cooled.

Nutritional Information (Per Serving)
Calories: 239; Fat: 3.7g; Net Carbohydrates: 47.1g; Protein: 5.3g

Oreo Cheesecake

Serves: 8
Preparation Time: 10 minutes
Cooking Time: 40 minutes
Ingredients for the Crust:
¼ cup melted butter
12 crushed and crumbled Oreo cookies

Ingredients for Oreo Cheesecake:
16 ounces cream cheese, room temperature
½ cup granulated sugar
2 large eggs, room temperature
1 tablespoon all-purpose flour
¼ cup heavy cream
2 teaspoons vanilla
8 whole Oreo cookies, coarsely chopped

Directions:
1. Cover the bottom and sides of a 7" springform pan with aluminum foil. Butter the inside of the pan.
2. In a bowl, mix the crumbled Oreo cookies with the melted butter.
3. Use your fingers to press the crumb mix to the bottom of the springform pan. Place pan with crust in the freezer for 15 minutes.
4. Use a mixer with a paddle attachment to whip the cream cheese until it is smooth. Combine with the sugar.
5. Add the eggs (must be at room temperature) and blend thoroughly.
6. Mix in the flour, cream, and vanilla and beat until the batter is smooth and creamy.
7. Stir in the chopped cookies.
8. Transfer the batter to the springform pan and cover with aluminum foil.
9. Insert a trivet into the Instant Pot and add 1½ cups of water.
10. Create a foil sling and place it on the trivet.

11. Set the springform pan on top of the foil and place the ends of the strips on top.

12. Cook at high pressure for 40 minutes.

13. When the cooking is complete, do a natural pressure release for 10 minutes. Quick release the remaining pressure.

14. Use the foil to lift the cake. Let cool.

15. Refrigerate the cheesecake for at least 8 hours.

Nutritional Information (Per Serving)
Calories: 450; Fat: 32.9g; Net Carbohydrates: 32.2g; Protein: 7.4g

Caramel Flan

Serves: 2
Preparation Time: 15 minutes
Cooking Time: 12 minutes
Ingredients:
For Caramel:
⅓ cup sugar
3 tablespoons water

For Flan:
2 eggs
1 egg yolk
3 tablespoons sugar
Pinch of salt
1 cup milk
¼ cup whipping cream
1 tablespoon hazelnut syrup
½ teaspoon vanilla extract

Directions:
1. *For caramel:* In a pan, add the sugar and water, heat over medium-high heat, and bring to a boil, stirring continuously. Cook until dark golden brown.

2. Carefully, place caramel into 2 (6-ounce) custard cups evenly. Keep aside to cool.

3. *For flan:* In a bowl, add the eggs, egg yolk, sugar, and salt and with a mixer, beat until well combined.

4. In a pan, add milk, and heat over medium heat until just warm.

5. Add warm milk to the egg mixture, beating continuously.

6. Add remaining ingredients and mix well.

7. Place custard into caramel-lined custard cups evenly. With the back of a spoon, remove all bubbles.

8. Arrange a steamer trivet in the Instant Pot. Add 1½ cups of water to the Instant Pot.

9. Place the custard cups on top of the trivet.

10. Secure the lid and cook at high pressure for 6 minutes.

11. When the cooking is complete, do a natural pressure release.

12. Remove the lid and transfer the custard cups onto a wire rack to cool.

13. With plastic wraps, cover the cups and refrigerate to chill for at least 4 hours before serving.

Nutritional Information (Per Serving)
Calories: 322; Fat: 14.1g; Net Carbohydrates: 40.7g; Protein: 0.2g

Apples A La Mode

Serves: 4
Preparation Time: 10 minutes
Cooking Time: 15 minutes
Ingredients:
4 red delicious apples
1 lemon
2 cups grape juice
¼ cup strawberry jelly
1 teaspoon pepper
½ vanilla bean
¼ cup crushed walnuts
4 cups ice cream

Directions:

1. Pour the juice and jelly into the Instant Pot. Set the pot to SAUTÉ, and heat while stirring until the jelly breaks down.

2. Grate the rind off the lemon then cut the lemon in half and squeeze the juice into the Instant Pot. Add the rind.

3. Core the apples from the bottom, so the form stays intact. Coat the apples in the jelly mixture and then wrap them in aluminum foil.

4. Place the apples in a steamer basket.

5. Add the pepper and vanilla to the pot and lower the apples. Cook for 10 minutes at high pressure.

6. When the cooking is complete, use a natural pressure release.

7. Unwrap the apples and cover them with ice cream and walnuts.

Nutritional Information (Per Serving)
Calories: 404; Fat: 12.2g; Net Carbohydrates: 66.2g; Protein: 5.6g

Chocolate Brownies

Serves: 12
Preparation Time: 10 minutes
Cooking Time: 35 minutes
Ingredients:
6 tablespoons unsalted butter
4 tablespoons unsweetened cocoa powder
1 cup sugar
¾ cup all-purpose flour
¼ teaspoon salt
¾ tablespoon baking powder
2 large eggs
¼ cup chopped walnuts
2 cups water

Directions:

1. In a small pan, melt the butter on the stove. Set aside and mix in the cocoa powder.
2. Mix the sugar, flour, salt, and baking powder in a small bowl. Add the eggs and walnuts and stir in the cocoa mix.
3. Transfer the batter to an 8" pan that's been greased. Use aluminum foil to cover.
4. Add the water to the Instant Pot and place the pan on a trivet.
5. Shut the lid and cook for 35 minutes at high pressure.
6. When the cooking is complete, use a natural pressure release.
7. Let brownies cool and cut into 2" squares.

Nutritional Information (Per Serving)
Calories: 175; Fat: 8.4g; Net Carbohydrates: 23.4g; Protein: 2.9g

Wine Poached Figs on Yogurt Crème

Serves: 4
Preparation Time: 10 minutes
Cooking Time: 7 minutes
Ingredients:
4 large sized figs
1 cup red wine
¼ cup honey
½ cup assorted nuts (chopped cashews, almonds, and pistachios)
4 cups plain yogurt

Directions:
1. Pour the yogurt into a mesh strainer and place it in the fridge to drain for about 6 hours. Do not wait for too long or the yogurt might get too crumbly.
2. Wash the figs and pat them dry. Place them in the Instant Pot. Add the wine and sugar and cover the lid of the pot.
3. Cook at high pressure for 6–7 minutes.
4. When the cooking is complete, use a natural pressure release.
5. On serving plates, add the yogurt crème, and poached figs. Garnish with wine syrup and chopped nuts on top.

Nutritional Information (Per Serving)
Calories: 433; Fat: 11.1g; Net Carbohydrates: 51.7g; Protein: 17.3g

Nutty Fudge Pieces

Yield: 2 dozen fudge pieces
Preparation Time: 10 minutes
Cooking Time: 5 minutes
Ingredients:
1 12-ounce package of semi-sweet chocolate chips
1 14-ounce can condensed milk
½ cup walnuts
½ cup almonds
1 teaspoon vanilla
2 cups water

Directions:
1. Combine the milk and chocolate chips in a bowl (make sure it will fit in your Instant Pot).
2. Cover the bowl with aluminum foil.
3. Pour the water into the Instant Pot and set a trivet so you can place the bowl on top of it.
4. Cook at high pressure for 5 minutes.
5. When the cooking is complete, use a natural pressure release.
6. Remove the bowl and take off the foil.
7. Stir in the nuts and vanilla until everything is combined.
8. Drop in unformed balls onto wax paper and allow to cool.

Nutritional Information (Per Fudge)
Calories: 157; Fat: 8.2g; Net Carbohydrates: 17.2g; Protein: 3.4g

Homemade Yogurt

Makes: 8 cups
Preparation Time: 10 minutes
Cooking Time: Up to 12 hours (fermentation) + 1 hour (boiling and cooling)
Ingredients:
8 cups whole milk
2 tablespoons plain yogurt with live active cultures (store-bought or from a previous batch)

Directions:
1. Add the milk to your Instant Pot. Close the lid, choose YOGURT, and adjust until you see the word "Boil" on the display. This will heat the milk to about 180°F.
2. Once the Instant Pot beeps, open the lid carefully and use a thermometer to check that the milk has reached at least 180°F. If not, use the "Sauté" function to heat, stirring constantly.
3. Remove the inner pot from the Instant Pot and allow the milk to cool to about 110°F. This usually takes about 30 minutes.
4. In a bowl, mix the 2 tablespoons of plain yogurt with a cup of the cooled milk. Whisk to combine. Add this mixture back to the inner pot and whisk to combine.
5. Place the inner pot back into the Instant Pot housing. Close the lid, choose YOGURT, and adjust the settings to ferment at 110°F for at least 4 hours. For tangier yogurt, you can ferment it for up to 12 hours.
6. Open the lid and gently stir the yogurt.
7. Divide the yogurt into sterilized jars, then place in the refrigerator for at least 4 hours to set and cool.
8. For flavored yogurt, add fresh fruits or fruit preserves.

Nutritional Information (Per 1 Cup Serving)
Calories: 155; Fat: 8.1g; Net Carbohydrates: 12.3g; Protein: 8.3g

Blueberry Walnut Porridge

Serves: 4
Preparation Time: 10 minutes
Cooking Time: 8 minutes
Ingredients:
1 cup steel-cut oats
2 cups water
1 cup almond milk
½ cup blueberries
¼ cup walnuts, chopped
½ teaspoon ground cinnamon
¼ teaspoon salt

Directions:
1. Add all ingredients to the Instant Pot. Stir to combine.
2. Close the lid, choose the MANUAL or PRESSURE COOK setting, and cook at high pressure for 8 minutes.
3. When the cooking is complete, do a natural pressure release for 10 minutes. Quick release the remaining pressure.
4. Drizzle honey or maple syrup over the top before serving.

Nutritional Information (Per Serving)
Calories: 142; Fat: 7.1g; Net Carbohydrates: 15.5g; Protein: 4.2g

Conclusion

I hope you enjoy the innovative recipes in this book. As you delve deeper into the world of Instant Pot cooking, may your days be filled with the comforting aroma of delightful dishes, the smiles of those you share them with, and the satisfaction of a meal well-cooked. Here's to many scrumptious meals and memories ahead!

Finally, I want to thank you for reading my book. If you enjoyed the book, please share your thoughts and post a review on the book retailer's website. It would be greatly appreciated!

Best wishes,
Angela Hopkins

www.ingramcontent.com/pod-product-compliance
Lightning Source LLC
Chambersburg PA
CBHW071240070526
44583CB00017B/2270